**BERLITZ®**

# MAJORCA

## and Minorca

1987/1988 Edition

D0773855

**By the staff of Berlitz Guides**
A Macmillan Company

**17th Printing**
**1988/1989 Edition**

# How to use our guide

- All the practical information, hints and tips that you will need before and during the trip start on page 95.

- For general background, see the sections Majorca and the Majorcans, p. 6, and A Brief History, p. 10.

- All the sights to see are listed between pages 20 and 71. Our own choice of sights most highly recommended is pin-pointed by the Berlitz traveller symbol.

- Entertainment, nightlife and all other leisure activities are described between pages 72 and 83 and from page 91 to 94, while information on restaurants and cuisine is to be found on pages 84 to 90.

- Finally, there is an index at the back of the book, pp. 126–128.

---

*Although we make every effort to ensure the accuracy of all the information in this book, changes occur incessantly. We cannot therefore take responsibility for facts, prices, addresses and circumstances in general that are constantly subject to alteration. Our guides are updated on a regular basis as we reprint, and we are always grateful to readers who let us know of any errors, changes or serious omissions they come across.*

---

Text and photography: Ken Welsh
We're particulary grateful to Mr. Charles W. Applegate, Mr. Philip J. Jerome, Mrs. Pilar Liman Rubio and to Miss Mercedes Martín Bartolomé of the Spanish National Tourist Office for their help in the preparation of this book.
Cartography: Falk Falk-Verlag, Hamburg.

# Contents

# Majorca and the Majorcans

Three million tourists can't be wrong. Every year they make Majorca the Mediterranean's most popular holiday island. They choose sun, sand and scenery—plus all the comfort and excitement anyone could ask for.

* The other principal islands in the group are Minorca, Ibiza and Formentera. In Spanish, Majorca is spelled *Mallorca,* and Minorca, *Menorca.*

The largest of Spain's Balearic islands,* Majorca is about 60 miles long and covers just 1,405 square miles—roughly the size of Cornwall in England, or of New York's Long Island. Within that area are two distinct regions, so you can switch from a beach holiday to the mountains, and back again, on the same day.

A majestic mountain chain almost five miles wide stretches from the southwestern tip of the island through to Cape Formentor at the ex-

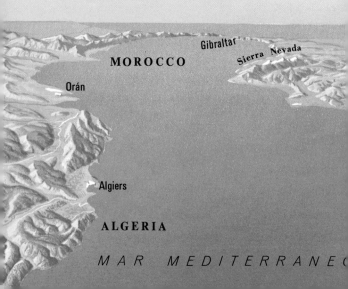

treme north. The 4,900-foot high Puig Mayor, the brooding pinnacle of the Balearic mountains, is often shrouded in mist.

Yet most of the island is a fertile plain, called Es Pla. Here the Majorcans grow their produce, irrigated by water drawn from seemingly limitless subterranean deposits. Geologists think the source may be high in the Pyrenees between France and Spain, the water reaching the island through undersea rock strata. It is drawn to the surface by hundreds of windmills—a striking feature you notice as your plane swoops in to land at Majorca's Son San Juan Airport.

The plain is also riddled with scores of caves and grottoes, some of which have been developed as tourist attractions.

But what draws the crowds to Majorca are the genuine Mediterranean climate and the coastline that winds around enticing bays, along

broad white-sand beaches and beneath breathtaking cliffs.

Tourism, agriculture and fishing are the economic backbone of the island. By way of light industry, Majorca produces shoes, artificial pearls, blown glass, furniture and textiles. (Some factories even invite tourists to watch the production processes.)

The mild climate and abundant water supply account for the great variety of fruit and vegetables grown in the fertile soil of Es Pla. The mountain chain is dotted with groves of olive trees, some a thousand years old. And in February, three million almond trees burst into blossom, filling the air with languid sweetness.

Spain is a multilingual nation. The Balearic islanders, as well as the Basques, Galicians and Catalans, have their own distinct languages or dialects but use Spanish as the unifying tongue.

The language of the Majorcans—a dialect of Catalan—is a vital aspect of their culture and character. During the Franco era, when regional tendencies were harshly suppressed, the Spanish language muscled aside *Mallorquí* (Majorcan) in all but family rela-

*A hint of garlic—few Majorcan dishes are complete without it.*

tions. Now the dialect has been restored to its place.

Majorcans relish their heritage in other ways. At weekends the citizens of Palma stream out to village inns in search of old-fashioned island delicacies, like *pa amb oli*, thick slabs of country bread, spread with olive oil, topped with fresh tomato and generous cuts of savoury mountain ham.

And on rainy nights (yes, there are some), if you see pinpricks of light moving across the fields, it's only respectable Majorcans out with their flash-lights in search of snails. The plump gasteropods, which surface in the rain, are used in a favourite, country speciality—snails with garlic and mayonnaise.

Aside from such diversions, the Majorcans are a hard-working and pragmatic people who harbour a tougher notion of life than many of their Spanish cousins. One Frenchman who lived on the island wrote of the Majorcans in awe: "Here children work like women, women work like men and men work like Titans."

But in one important respect Majorcans are very much like mainland Spaniards. They are open, friendly and curious about you. It's easy to strike up an acquaintance so don't hesitate to try out at least one word of Majorcan.

*Silvered leaves make unusual street decorations at Valldemossa fiesta.*

# A Brief History

The origins of the Balearic people and the traces of their complicated prehistoric civilizations lie literally along the side of the road in the form of mysterious stone relics. Stop your car at Capocorp Vell on Majorca (page 37) or at any of a hundred sites on Minorca (pages 67 and 68) and see for yourself. Here you will find ponderous stone structures called *talaiots*. One theory claims they were used for burials, another that they were simply cocoon-like defensive living quarters. In any case, they have given their name to the first period in Balearic history—the Talaiot.

The people who built these remarkably indestructible monuments are thought to have been offshoot tribes of the Iberian race from North Africa and the northern European Celts. These two peoples came to Spain around 3,000 B.C. and merged to become the Celtiberians.

One of their descendants' peculiar skills was the deadly

*Fierce island slingers, unequalled in their art, kept their foes at bay.*

use of the sling, which effectively held off a succession of invaders. This skill may have given the islands their name: some believe Balearic comes from the Greek *ballein,* meaning to throw.

In the 3rd century B.C., Majorca and Minorca were captured by the Carthaginians, heirs to the ancient Phoenician empire. As far back as the 5th century B.C., the Carthaginians had established trading ports at Málaga and Cádiz. The leader of the Carthaginian invasion was Hamilcar Barca, after whom the Catalan capital of Barcelona is named. Barca's son, Hannibal, was later to achieve even greater fame than his father.

The Romans defeated the Carthaginians in 146 B.C., but the islanders continued to harass the Roman fleets. In 123 B.C., exasperated by these attacks, the Romans launched an invasion of the islands under Quintus Caecilius Metellus.

Even with the aid of the feared Balearic slingers, the

*Frieze commemorating Jaime I's successful invasion of Majorca in 1229.*

islanders' defence was doomed, because Metellus' ships were shielded by hides to ward off the hail of stone missiles.

Once in possession, the Romans gave the islands their present names: *Balearis Major* which has become Majorca, and *Balearis Minor*, Minorca.

The Roman conquest of the islands succeeded in clearing the Balearic waters of pirates, who were disrupting Mediterranean trade-routes, and added the resources of the islands to the rapidly expanding empire.

Rome brought political stability and her Latin culture to the peninsula and the islands. She built such cities as Seville, Córdoba and Mérida on the mainland and Palma and Alcùdia on Majorca. She built roads, aqueducts and monuments and gave the country the language that is the origin of present-day Catalan and Spanish.

But as the unwieldy and changing empire began to decline and as political instability in Rome left the colonies more and more on their own, succeeding waves of invaders managed to supplant Roman power. Vandals and Goths, for example, both had their moments in Spain and in the Balearics.

## The Tide of Islam

By A.D. 711 the second great invasion which was to alter the structure of Iberian civilization was gathering momentum on the nearby continent of Africa.

The Moslem religion has swept like a desert wind across the lands inhabited by the Arab people. Among the converts was a warlike, nomadic

*Bronze statue of war-god Mars unearthed at site near San Favar.*

Photo: Mascaró Pasarius

North African tribe, the Moors. Their name derives from Mauretania, the Roman name for present-day Morocco. The Moors were determined to carry their new Islamic faith into Europe and invaded Spain by way of Gibraltar.

They defeated a Visigoth army near Tarifa and within 10 years had conquered most of the country. They then crossed the Pyrenees and penetrated deep into France before being defeated by the Frankish leader Charles Martel at Poitiers in 732.

Under Islam, the Iberian peninsula eventually became an independent caliphate with its capital in Córdoba. The city's population grew almost to one million inhabitants, and Córdoba became one of the major centres of scholarship in Europe.

In 902 the Moors turned their attention to the Balearics. They conquered Majorca and launched a series of raids against Minorca. Early in the 10th century, the smaller island was finally conquered and, along with Majorca, brought under the banner of the caliphate of Córdoba. Shortly thereafter, the caliphate splintered into a group of 20 independent kingdoms, and from time to time various rulers annexed the islands to their domains, until 1127 when Majorca became an independent kingdom.

## The Reconquest

As the spirit of the Crusades developed, medieval Christianity was not prepared to tolerate Moslems on "Christian" territory, be it in Jerusalem or in Spain. Within the latter, Christian enclaves were forging alliances that would launch them on the road to the Reconquest *(la Reconquista)*, a sporadic series of battles, treaties, sieges and still more battles, that lasted in all more than five centuries, before the Moors were expelled.

The Christians finally returned to Majorca in September, 1229, with an army of 16,000 men and 1,500 horses, transported in more than 150 ships. The leader of this formidable expedition was Jaime I of Aragón—James the Conqueror.

The army landed at the present-day resort of Santa Ponsa on September 10 and was engaged by 18,000 defenders. A 13

*Hero of the* Reconquista, *Jaime I expelled the Moors from Majorca.*

series of skirmishes, followed by the siege of Palma, culminated on December 31, when the walls of the city were breached and the city fell to the Christians. Jaime then established the independent (and Christian) kingdom of Majorca.

The Moors of Minorca, on the other hand, agreed in 1232 to pay tribute to Aragón (4,500 bushels of wheat and 600 head of cattle) and were left in peace. However, when the Moorish governor warned North African towns of an imminent Christian invasion, that was regarded as treason. King Alfonso III of Aragón raised an army and conquered the island in 1287.

The Moors were suffering similar setbacks all over the peninsula. In 1212, their defeat in the decisive battle of Navas de Tolosa in northern Andalusia had shattered their hold over the Iberian peninsula. Gradually they retreated until all that remained was the kingdom of Granada. Here they held on for nearly 300 years of intermittent peace and war, while the Christian forces coalesced into fewer but larger political units.

Majorca, at the time an independent kingdom under Jaime III, was attacked by Pedro IV of Aragón. When Jaime died at Llucmajor in 1349, the island was annexed to the kingdom of Aragón.

Under Ferdinand and Isabella, the renowned Catholic Monarchs, who, by their marriage, united Aragón and Castile, the final scene in the epic of the Reconquest was set. The combined army marched against Moorish Granada, which finally fell to the Christians in 1492.

For the first time in its history, a united Spain faced the future.

## The Golden Age

As one age was ending, another was beginning. At Santa Fe, the town Isabella and Ferdinand had built during the siege of Granada, the monarchs met with Christopher Columbus, the Genoan sailor who believed he could find a new route to the East by sailing west. In 1492, the same year that Granada fell, Columbus reached the Caribbean islands.

His feat marked the beginning of a century during which Spain exported its adventurers, traders and priests, its language, culture and religion to the New World. And from there, the *conquistadores,* men like Pizarro and Cortés, sent back shiploads of silver and gold, incalculable riches that transformed Spain's position in European politics.

But the wealth from the

*Palma's illustrious son, Ramón Llull, doctor, theologian, poet.*

New World remained in relatively few hands; it neither benefited the mass of the people nor was it used to strengthen and expand the country's economy. Moreover, Spain's political and territorial ambitions, expressed in endless wars in Europe and the New 15

*Infamous May 3, 1808, executions under Napoleon, depicted by Goya.*

World, drained her of wealth and manpower. One crushing blow was the destruction of her "invincible" Armada of ships attempting to land an army in England in 1588.

Majorca, too, had her share of troubles. While building a fine commercial fleet and developing strong trading links around the Mediterranean, Majorca and Minorca were continually harassed by North African and Turkish pirates. So numerous and destructive were the raids that many of Majorca's port towns had to be rebuilt safely inland. Thus, today, Alcùdia is twinned with Puerto Alcùdia and Pollensa with Puerto Pollensa.

## French Ascendancy

During the wars in Europe in the following century, Spanish internal affairs became the concern of other great powers, especially France. The daughter of Ferdinand and Isabella had married the son and heir of the Holy Roman Emperor, Maximilian of Hapsburg. After the death of the Catholic Monarchs, the Spanish crown had passed to the Hapsburgs and remained in Hapsburg hands until the demise of Charles II, who died without an heir in 1700. The War of the Spanish Succession (1702-13) brought Philippe de Bourbon of France to the Spanish throne.

Nearly a hundred years later, Spanish ships fought alongside Napoleon's fleet against Adm. Horatio Nelson at Trafalgar in 1805. But as the war dragged on, Napoleon became distrustful of his Spanish ally, forcibly replaced the king of Spain with his own brother, Joseph Bonaparte, and then sent an army to subdue the country and to move against Britain's ally, Portugal. The Spaniards resisted, and, aided by British troops under the command of the Duke of Wellington, they drove the French from the Iberian peninsula. What we know as the Peninsular War (1808–14) is referred to in Spain as the War of Independence, and Spain's first constitution was drafted during that period.

*The man who put Majorca on the map, Archduke Ludwig Salvator.*

## Chaos and Decline

But hopes of setting up a constitutional monarchy were rapidly dashed, and Spain was plunged into a century of power struggles. Overseas, its American colonies revolted and gained independence. The last Spanish possessions to go—Cuba, Puerto Rico and the Philippines—were eventually lost through American intervention. In 1902, Alfonso XIII, a young man of only 16, took up his duties as king.

After an embarrassing defeat by local rebels in Morocco, the king accepted a general, Primo de Rivera, as dictator in 1923. Six years later the general fell. Neither reform nor maintenance of order seemed possible. In 1931, the king himself went into exile following anti-royalist election results, and a Spanish republic was founded.

As a parliamentary democracy, with a succession of right-wing attempts to govern, Spain floundered in a sea of 17 political strikes and violence. Each party was ideologically committed; compromise was rare. The political scene became chaotic, and assassinations were frequent.

## Civil War and Peace

In 1936, a large section of the army under General Francisco Franco, supported by the monarchists, conservatives, the clergy and the right-wing Falange, rose against the government.

On the government side against them were republicans, liberals, socialists, communists and anarchists. The ensuing civil war became one of the major conflicts of the 20th century, with much support for both sides coming from outside Spain. To many people in Europe, often unaware of or indifferent to the particular Spanish origins of the struggle, it was seen as a crucial battle between democracy and dictatorship, or, from the other side, as one between law and order and the forces of social revolution and chaos. The war lasted three years, cost more than 500,000 lives and sent large numbers of Spaniards into exile. Majorca and Minorca did not escape—the islands suffered through both land battles and air-raids, though on a lesser scale than many places in mainland Spain.

An exhausted Spain was able to stay on the sidelines in the Second World War. In the postwar years, the tough law-and-order regime of Franco set in motion the nation's recovery. Then came the phenomenon of mass tourism, with profound effects on the economy and the people.

Franco's designated successor, the grandson of Alfonso XIII, was enthroned on the death of the dictator in 1975. To the dismay of Franco's followers, King Juan Carlos I flung open the gates to democracy. After years of repression, the languages and cultures of the Balearic Islands, Catalonia and the Basque Country enjoyed a renaissance, and regional autonomy was granted.

Firmly back in the mainstream after its long isolation, democratic Spain hitched its future to the European Community.

*Burgeoning demand for hand-made souvenirs revives ancient crafts.*

# Where to Go

Don't be misled by that word "island"—though you may never be more than an hour's drive from the sea, and can discover a new beach every day, Majorca's 1,250 miles of roads also provide access to a varied, fascinating interior.

Start sightseeing at Palma, capital of all the Balearic islands, which offers everything you're likely to want from a big city—shopping, sightseeing, amusements.

Then, for more restful times, visit some of the charming villages off the beaten track. Scramble over prehistoric or Roman ruins, see some of Spain's finest caves, or take to the wooded hills.

For a holiday within a holiday, try a 20-minute flight to the Catalonian capital of Barcelona*. Or, for a more restful break, hop onto a ferryboat for Minorca (pages 61–71) or Ibiza*.

---

*In this same series, Berlitz has published travel guides devoted entirely to Barcelona and the Costa Dorada and to Ibiza and Formentera.

*Main road to Sa Calobra winds through man-made cleft in rock.*

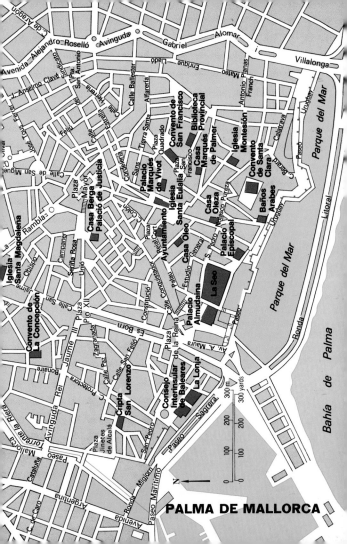

PALMA DE MALLORCA

## Palma de Mallorca
Pop. 305,000

Lucky travellers see it first by boat. Dead ahead: the city's famed Gothic cathedral with the ancient Almudaina Palace beneath. Over to the right: glimpses of the long, white beaches of Ca'n Pastilla and El Arenal, known jointly as Playa de Palma. To the left: the sweep of Spain's most elegant seaside promenade with its luxury hotels and yacht harbour. And crowning all, the white, circular battlements of Bellver Castle.

Nearly two-thirds of the total population of Majorca lives in Palma, making it by far the largest city in all the Balearics. The crowd is swelled by visitors from cruise ships and men-of-war anchored in the bay and by tourists commuting from nearby resorts for a day's shopping and sightseeing. Thus Palma has earned its reputation as one of the most bustling and cosmopolitan cities in the Mediterranean.

Any exploration of Palma logically begins at the lively, tree-shaded central paseo known as **Es Born**. This elongated plaza almost at the foot of the Almudaina Palace, once the scene of jousting tournaments, is now the hub of the city's social life. All day, tourists and businessmen meet over coffee or drinks at the many cafés lining the plaza. In the evening, the tree-lined central promenade comes alive with strolling couples. On each side old men sit on stone

benches reliving memories in the fading light.

At the top of the Born is **Avinguda Rei Jaume III,** Majorca's most exclusive thoroughfare. The sleek, expensive shops and offices symbolize the new sophistication of a city grown rich from tourism.

The **Palacio Almudaina** itself was once the residence of the Moorish kings. After the Reconquest it was rebuilt and used by the kings of Majorca. Completely restored in 1963 according to the original plans, the palace now serves as the headquarters of the Cap-

*Palma's Gothic cathedral—celebrated landmark in exotic palm setting.*

tain-General of Majorca. In the wing open to the public, you can see Flemish tapestries illustrating Spanish history, standards from the titanic naval battle of Lepanto (1571) in which a Turkish fleet was soundly defeated by Spanish and Venetian galleys, portraits of the long-dead Majorcan kings and the 16th-century chapel of St. Anne.

In the gardens of S'Hort del Rei, in front of the palace, stands a mobile called *Nancy*, donated to Palma by the American sculptor Alexander Calder. Islanders and visitors alike hotly dispute the appropriateness of such a work here.

One of Spain's best-known landmarks, the massive Gothic **cathedral** *(La Seo)*, overshadows the delicately arched and covered balconies of the palace. According to legend, King Jaime I was caught off Majorca in a terrible storm in 1229. In mortal danger, he swore that if he were saved he would build a church dedicated to St. Mary. He survived and donated the 75,000 square feet of land the cathedral now covers. The edifice itself wasn't completed until 1601. In the sacristy, the cathedral treasure includes hand-

*Remains of Arab Baths reflect superiority of Moorish artistry.*

painted manuscripts, a jewel-studded crucifix and bone fragments said to come from the skeletons of saints. The kings of Majorca (Jaime II and Jaime III) are buried here.

Close by, in the **Palacio Episcopal** in Calle del Palau, the Diocesan Museum displays objects as curious and diverse as Malayan daggers, the sword hilt of the last king of Poland, icons, ceramics, Roman coins and Queen Victoria's autograph.

Palma is also a city of *barrios,* or distinctive quarters. One of the most fascinating to visit, for both history and architecture, is the barrio Portella, directly behind the cathedral.

Here you can see the only Arab monuments in the city surviving in their original form: the **Almudaina Arch** *(Arco de Almudaina)* in Calle Almudaina and the **Arab Baths** *(Baños Arabes)* in Calle Serra. But the main attractions in the narrow streets of Portella are its ancient baronial **mansions,** some dating from the 15th century. Glimpses into the cool, stone patios of Palma's "stately homes" give a hint of an aristocratic life-style on the verge of extinction.

For a closer look visit the **Palacio Vivot.** This magnificent example of aristocratic Majorcan architecture, residence of the Marqués de Vivot, has been declared a national monument and opened to the public. To enter, go through the court-

*The Palacio Vivot—a sumptuous museum of Majorcan nobility.*

yard at 2, Calle de Zavella. (It's also numbered Casa 3.) You'll have to tug at a chain to ring the bell. You will be admitted into a flamboyant, baroque world which contrasts dramatically with the palace's severe Gothic exterior. The highly personal tour introduces you to a sumptuous collection of paintings, tapestries, silver, old maps and antique furniture, all heirlooms of the Vivot family.

Only a few steps away from the Palacio Vivot is the 14th-century **Convent of St. Francis** *(Convento de San Francisco),* which has been declared a national monument. The body of Ramón Llull (or, as he was 25

*El Consejo's former defences, now hobby-horses for youngsters.*

dubbed in Latin, Raimundus Lullus), Majorca's great 13th-century philosopher-priest, rests in the convent.

Llull, after enjoying a wild and debauched youth, lost a lady-love and turned to religion. He wrote some 250 books on theology, philosophy and poetry and set out to convert all of Islam to Christianity.

The convent's Gothic **cloister,** built between the 14th and 15th centuries, displays a strong Moorish influence. In the middle stands a charming garden with a 17th-century well.

Stroll westwards to the Born and then head towards the seafront. There you'll come to a statue of Llull. Near the statue

is the Paseo Sagrera, the beginning of Palma's delightful Paseo Marítimo (seaside promenade). Here, side by side, stand two of the capital's most important buildings: La Lonja and El Consejo Interinsular de Baleares.

**La Lonja,** built in the first half of the 15th century by the Majorcan architect Guillermo Sagrera (after whom the *paseo* is named), is considered one of Spain's finest secular Gothic buildings. This squat, turreted building was once Palma's trade-exchange centre but in recent years has become a museum of Balearic art, with works dating back to the 14th century.

**El Consejo Interinsular de Baleares** (Inter-Island Balearic Council), an elegant Renaissance-style structure, was built in the 17th century by the merchants' guild. Here, captains came to register ships and cargo, buy licences and settle differences under maritime law. The Consejo, with cannons and a huge anchor in front, houses the autonomous Balearic Island government.

Surrounding these buildings, dozens of palm trees reach whimsically skywards. The trees, after which the city of Palma was named, are said to have been introduced from Africa during the long Arab occupation.

Farther down the *paseo,* in the harbour, million-dollar ocean-going yachts, flying the colours of far-off lands, contrast with dinghies belonging to weekend sailors. The workaday but nonetheless romantic world of the deep-sea fishing fleet may be seen at the fishermen's wharf. On gaudily painted boats and ashore, leather-skinned salts tend to the never-ending maintenance of their nets and equipment.

The buildings around the Born and the magnificent promenade may be Palma's most obvious attractions, but other areas of this old city contain no end of surprises.

Plunge into the real-life excitement of the central **market** *(mercado)* at Plaza Olivar. Take in the drama of strident housewives competing with even noisier vendors staged before a backdrop of tons of fresh fruits and vegetables. Don't miss the display of deep-sea wonders in the seafood section—from prawns to mighty swordfish and tunny (tuna).

On your way to or from the

*Pedestrians-only zones add to shopping and window-gazing ease.*

market you can visit more of Palma's landmarks: the stately 17th-century town hall *(Ayuntamiento)* in Plaza Cort and, about halfway between the town hall and the market, the recently reconstructed Plaza Mayor, the original city market centre.

27

*Haggling can be fun and profitable in Palma's popular gypsy market.*

On Saturday mornings, head for the outdoor flea market centered on Avinguda Gabriel Alomar i Villalonga. Serious junk-rakers, ever hopeful of finding an original Goya for 100 pesetas, can delve into a treasure trove stretching almost a mile. Hawkers assure you with exquisite mournfulness that they accidentally sell a masterpiece once a month. Who knows what you may be holding in your hand? Remember to bargain furiously.

In the seedy **Barrio de San Antonio** local colour flourishes in the late-night hours. Palma's mini red-light district is another reminder of the city's reputation as a cosmopolitan port.

For exciting night-life of a more ordinary sort, head west to the beachside suburb of **El Terreno.** White villas, long the haunts of retired foreigners, line the steep streets behind Avenida Joan Miró. But around the central **Plaza Gomila** you can choose among dozens of restaurants, cafés, neon-lit bars and noisy discotheques.

For the full flavour of throbbing El Terreno take one of the outdoor tables around 10 p.m. Order a long drink and observe the scene: thousands of holiday-makers and Majorcans packing the square in search of action and pleasure.

Halfway between El Terreno and Palma and behind the Paseo Marítimo, is the area known as **El Jonquet.** Here, in a bohemian atmosphere reminiscent of Paris' Montmartre, you find some of the island's most famous night-spots. A couple have been built into ancient windmills which once ground the city's corn. On a clear night the view of Palma's bay is stunning: a flood-lit cathedral, a fairy-light-spangled ocean liner.

Day-time El Terreno is hard to relate to the dazzle of its night-time existence. It suf-

28

fers a perpetual hangover, battling to recharge its energies for yet another night of fun. But high above, a sturdy symbol of the island never changes. **Bellver Castle** *(Castillo de Bellver),* standing at 450 feet above sea-level in pine-wooded Bellver Park, has commanded sea and land approaches to the city since it was built in the 14th century by order of Jaime II of Majorca. The castle is one of the finest examples anywhere of 14th- and 15th-century mili-

*High above Palma, Bellver Castle still stands guard after 600 years.*

tary architecture. Yet, this circular structure of golden stone has a strangely modern look.

Once the summer retreat of the Majorcan kings, in more recent centuries the castle has served as a jail for criminals and political prisoners. See the dungeons in the Tower of

*Replicas of Spanish architecture on view at the Pueblo Español.*

Homage; visit the museum for its modest display of armour and furniture; and then take in the view over Palma from the battlements.

Another Palma excursion covers the **Pueblo Español** (Spanish village). This outdoor museum, between Palma and El Terreno, features many scaled-down replicas of Spain's most celebrated architectural treasures. From the glories of Granada's Alhambra to the soaring beauty of Seville's Giralda Tower, you can "see Spain in a day" within the walls of the Pueblo Español. It's nearly enough to make you hop on a plane to the mainland.

Surrounded by the history, culture and glamour of Palma, don't fail to miss an equally impressive side of Majorca. A world of glancing shadows and crumbling, textured walls awaits tourists venturing off the main thoroughfares. Sidestep early morning shoppers in crowded alleys. Elbow your way into workers' cafés and taverns. Here you'll find the Palma which will burn into your mind and remind you of the island long after memories of castles and cathedrals are gone.

# The Bay of Palma

Palma's playground is a massive crescent of white sand—from swinging Magaluf on the western end to brash El Arenal on the east—embracing the blue-green waters of a magnificent bay. Magaluf and El Arenal are affectionately dubbed the Terrible Two by holiday-makers who return season after season. Here is a brief description of what lies between these points.

*Santa Ponsa: Reconquista army's beachhead is now a tourist mecca.*

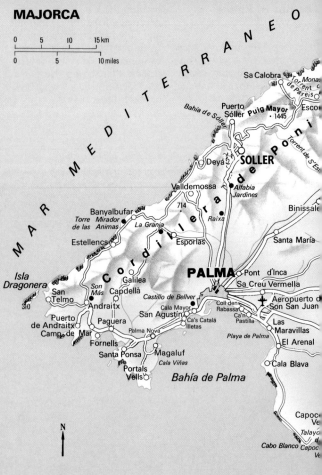

# MAJORCA

0   5   10   15 km

0   5   10 miles

MAR   MEDITERRANEO

Sa Calobra
Monat
de Pareis
Esc
Torrent de Pareis
Bahía de Sóller
Puerto
Sóller   Puig Mayor · 1445
Torrent de s'Es
SOLLER
Deyá
Cordillera de Ponl
Valldemossa   Alfabia
Jardines
Binissalè
714
Banyalbufar
Torre   Mirador   La Granja   Raixa
de las   de las Animas
Animas
Estellencs   Santa María
Esporlas
Isla
Dragonera   Cordillera   PALMA   Pont d'Inca
Son   Galilea   Sa Creu Vermella
San   Más   Capdellà
Telmo   Castillo de Bellver   Aeropuerto d
310   Andraitx   Coll den   Son San Juan
Rabassa
Puerto   Cala Mayor   Ca'n
de Andraitx   Paguera   San Agustín   Pastilla   Las
Camp de Mar   Ca's Catalá   Maravillas
Palma Nova   Illetas   Playa de Palma   El Arenal
Fornells
Santa Ponsa   Magaluf   Cala Blava
Portals   Cala Viñas
Vells   Bahía de Palma
Capoc
Ve
N   Talayo
d
Cabo Blanco Capoc
Ve

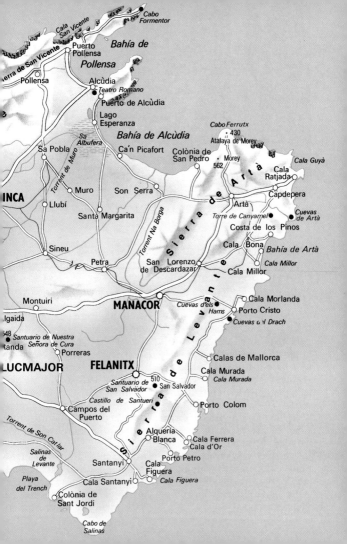

*Generation gap or cultural shock? Majorca has room for wide variety.*

## WEST FROM PALMA

CALA MAYOR (great cove) is so close to the centre of Palma that it was an obvious area for tourist development long before the invention of the package tour. Even the royal family has used Cala Mayor as a base for sailing holidays. It's heavily booked in season, as is SAN AGUSTÍN just to the west.

At ILLETAS the beaches are small but the scenery—steep, wooded hillsides descending to attractive coves—more than compensates for their size. Three tiny islands just off-shore gave Illetas, meaning islets, its name.

The next of the string of resorts on the road out of Palma is PORTALS NOUS. The beach is small, but there are opportunities for adventurous swimming from nearby rocks. During the 13th century, Moorish prisoners quarried stone from Portals Nous to build Palma's cathedral.

PALMA NOVA and neighbouring MAGALUF comprise an impressive resort complex developed along some three miles of desirable beach backed by rugged pine-covered hills. Ranks of high-rise hotels and apartment blocks have emerged from the emptiness during the last 20 years; there had never been so

*Recipe for a Majorcan speciality: ten minutes on each side, then baste...*

much as a village here. For thousands of sun-seekers this is exactly the Mediterranean dream come true—the sand, swimming, climate, luxurious facilities for the whole family and happy crowds of like-minded holiday-makers living it up alongside one another. It's only about 15 kilometres to Palma by bus. For a more relaxing trip, you can go by boat.

In absolute contrast to the hustle and bustle of this resort development is PORTALS VELLS on the southern tip of this side of the island. The sandy beach at the end of the small cove here is best reached by boat.

## EAST FROM PALMA

CA'N PASTILLA, one of the most heavily built-up resort areas, is only a couple of miles from the runway of Son San Juan Airport. The sight of the beach from arriving planes is enough to make many a passenger wish he could unfasten his seat belt and take a short-cut to a swim. The yacht harbour here can berth more than 500 boats.

The two-mile-long stretch of beach from Ca'n Pastilla through LAS MARAVILLAS and EL ARENAL is crowded with more than its share of the island's 2,000 hotels. But holiday-makers don't come to this 35 part of the world for solitude.

Yet there's always space on the beach for one more, and finding your spot can have delightful sequels as you daintily step around the very prime of European youth. If you happen to trip over a basking body, don't worry. You'll soon find that the language barrier—be it Swedish, German or French—is not really so formidable.

On this Majorcan riviera the fun continues far into the night. You can eat German sausages, English fish and chips, Danish open sandwiches or Spanish-style deep-fried squid. See a flamenco show, go wild in a disco or dance cheek-to-cheek to music from the '40s.

*"Tea like mum makes"*, one English café announces. Elsewhere: *"Hablamos español con acento—Wir sprechen Deutsch, eins zwei saufen—We speak English, jolly good show—Vi taler Svenska sa mycket bra för er"* and so on in a dozen languages, ending, *"Sign language accepted just in case"*.

And if the fun gets a little forced, the neon too bright, the music too loud? Just around the Punta Aranol, about four kilometres away, is the strangely tranquil CALA BLAVA. Swim out far enough from the *cala*'s rocks, float on your back, and you can just hear—if you try very hard —the sound of thousands of holiday-makers all having a good time.

*Every island town and village has ample table space for thirsty tourists.*

# Around Majorca's Coast

Even the most tireless tourist won't have time to visit all the high spots around the varied coast of Majorca. Here we suggest some sights you may find worthy of excursions. We've arranged them in anti-clockwise order starting from Palma. In each case the distances shown are from Palma.

## CAPOCORP VELL
*(Palma, 37 km)*

After the boisterous bay area, the region beyond Cala Blava comes as a balmy back-to-nature contrast. After a few scattered housing developments, the wild coastal land is streaked with low stone walls and dotted with stunted, wind-blown pines. At some spots you can drive to the edge of the cliff to pause and survey the sheer 200-foot precipices of CABO BLANCO with the ocean stretching away into an infinity of dazzling reflections.

The road then heads inland for slightly more than six kilometres to the hamlet of CAPO-CORP VELL, which has existed on this spot since 1,000 B.C. The extensive remains of the original **Bronze Age settlement** are surrounded by a wall with a locked gate. The gate-keeper lives at the 500-year-old farm-house nearby (a worthwhile visit in itself).

Amateur archaeologists should take the opportunity to wander over the ruins of dozens of houses, the site of a crematorium and two *talaiots* (see page 10). Agile explorers can crawl down a winding, pitch-black tunnel to the base of the bigger tower. The tunnel may have been the burial place of village chieftains.

*Tunnels lead to the Bronze Age at Capocorp Vell's prehistoric site.*

## CALA FIGUERA
*(Palma, 69 km)*

Rich farm country lies between Capocorp Vell and Cala Figuera. Here creaking windmills, pumping water from wells dug a thousand years ago by the Arabs, irrigate the land. In barnyards, cows, pigs, goats, caged rabbits and free-roaming chickens supply meat and dairy produce. Close by, farmers till their fields with tractors or wooden ploughs pulled by oxen. The open-air circular stone floors behind some houses were once used for threshing and milling corn.

About halfway between Capocorp Vell and Cala Figuera, the fishing village of COLÒNIA DE SANT JORDI is blossoming into a resort. Nearby, the Salinas de Levante (salt-flats of the east) are haunted by island ornithologists using high-powered binoculars and telephoto lenses to observe and photograph migrating birds. Following the road northeast from Colònia de Sant Jordi brings you to SANTANYI. Casually sign-posted streets lead you to the island's most beautiful seaside town, **Cala Figuera**—the village known as the Venice of Majorca.

The *cala* (cove) cuts into the coast, then turns and narrows into a long tongue of completely sheltered water. On either side of the inlet, and built nearly to the edge, are the houses of the fishing families who have lived here for centuries. The children play along the narrow footpaths and jetties with the sea literally on the doorstep.

Here you'll find houses with garages for boats, not cars. Slip-rails and pulley systems guide the boats in and out of the sea. Anchored at the cove's entrance is the deep-sea fleet, the mainstay of the village's economy.

## CALA D'OR
*(Palma, 77 km)*

One get-away-from-it-all spot between Cala Figuera and Cala d'Or is the fishing village of PORTO PETRO. The small bay is an ideal place to learn

*Figuera—reminiscences of Venice.* Left: *fisherman mends his nets.*

sailing. The loose string of cafés and shops along the harbour front provides just enough amenities.

Nearby CALA D'OR is a classic Majorcan holiday resort. Modern concrete-and-glass hotels and cubed, Ibiza-style villas climb the hillside from the clean sands and clear, green waters. This fashionable spot, long a favourite of islanders themselves, retains an aura of exclusivity which charms year-round foreign residents.

*A hired boat will in no time whisk you far away from noisy crowds.*

## PORTO CRISTO
*(Palma, 60 km)*

The Italians wouldn't agree. Neither would most historians. But in the lazy fishing port of PORTO COLOM, legend claims that the town was the birthplace of Christopher Colombus. While no documents prove the Majorcan claim, local pundits like to point out that Genoa—Columbus' usually accepted hometown—can't produce much evidence either. And, they say, at least Porto Colom is named after its alleged local boy.

Between Porto Colom and Porto Cristo, isolated beaches await in nearly 20 coves. The crowds are kept away by the topography. Getting there means taking bumpy roads or dusty tracks. But even here, in the high season, you won't feel like a hermit. On this undeveloped coast, CALA MURADA is a quiet resort with a few hotels and lots of summer houses.

PORTO CRISTO, about 18 kilometres up the coast, thrives as a quiet but well-equipped family resort. The 200-yard-long beach with its shallow water is ideal for children. A short walk away, in the fishermen's harbour, you can watch the catch arriving just after sunrise. Further fishy pursuits await at the aquarium, just behind the centre of town. And, north, lies the Safari Park (see p. 83).

Two caves near Porto Cristo are especially popular with tourists. You may want to see one or both either in making a circuit of the island or on a day's excursion from where you are staying.

Majorca is famous for its caves. It's so riddled with them that one Spanish saint, Vicente Ferrer, claimed the island was hollow. He prophesied that the heat of the fire of local sin would one day crack the crust of the land; the island, sinners and all, would then be swallowed by the sea.

The popular **Cuevas del Drach** (caves of the dragon) attract thousands of visitors every day during the summer. Discovered at the end of the last century, they lie 75 feet above sea level and stretch for more than a mile. A two-hour guided tour takes in expertly lit, fanciful shapes with names like the Ruined Castle, the Fairy's Theatre and Diana's Bath.

But the highlight is at **Lago Martel,** a stretch of perfectly 41

*The Cuevas del Drach are among the most visited grottoes in the world.*

still water 581 feet long by 98 feet wide, reaching a depth of 46 feet. This underground lake is named after a leading French speleologist, E. A. Martel, who with two companions explored the cave in 1896.

In the huge cavern facing the lake a thousand people can witness an unforgettable subterranean spectacle. The lights dim, and for one anxious moment there is total darkness. Then, gradually, pinpoints of light appear over the lake, and three boats silently glide into view. In one craft a floating trio—of violin, cello and organ—play overwrought classics reminiscent of the extravaganzas of Hollywood's Golden Age.

The **Cuevas de Hams** (caves of the hooks) show nature in a more whimsical mood. The tiny, exquisite caves are said to be unique. In one small cavern stalagmites and stalactites have grown like branches and twigs of trees—or like hooks. These seemingly impossible shapes have been formed by centuries of dripping water fanned by vagrant air currents.

Not much happens in the tiny resorts of CALA MORLANDA, S'ILLOT and CALA MOREYA, except that the sun rises each morning. By 10.30 a.m. in summer the white beaches are baking, enticement enough for many refugees from northern European cities.

Nearby CALA MILLOR is a quite different story. The three-mile crescent of sand is spattered with a dazzling patchwork of parasols. Between the beach and the hotels and apartment blocks, a traffic-free promenade attracts strolling crowds. Tourists from the quiet neighbouring resort of CALA BONA wander a mile along the beach-front to Cala Millor when they crave excitement. In winter, both resorts change dramatically. Restaurants and bars are shuttered, and Cala Bona's small fishing fleet again becomes the area's only industry.

## CALA RATJADA
*(Palma, 80 km)*

COSTA DE LOS PINOS means "pine coast". The stunted, windswept trees straggle down from the hills right to the edge of the beach, the sharp smell of their resin filling the air. The nearby **Torre de Canyamel,** an old fortified Gothic tower, was built as a defence against pirate attack. This scenic area is the setting for a nine-hole golf course.

The **Cuevas de Artà** (caves of Artà) were named after an ancient inland town (see page

*Back to the light of day from the underworld of the Cuevas de Artà.*

44). The massive entrance, cut into the coastal cliffs, gapes like some mythical gateway to hell. One visitor to the caves, Jules Verne, was said to have been impressed by the tortured shapes of its stalagmites and stalactites, drawing upon these impressions when he wrote *Journey to the Centre of the Earth.*

CALA RATJADA is the farthest point on the island from Palma. Once only a cluster of fishermen's houses, it's now a first-class holiday village with abundant restaurants and nightlife. Close by are the excellent beaches of CALA GUYA and CALA MOLTO. For striking views of the coast, walk up to the lighthouse on rocky Punta 43 des Farayes. From there you can also see Mount Jaumell (altitude 889 feet), where, before the days of submarine cables, a semaphore signalling station maintained visual communication with the island of Minorca, about 25 miles away.

A favourite visit from Cala Ratjada takes in CAPDEPERA, where the ruins of a 14th-century castle still stand guard on a hilltop above the town. Legend says that once, when Capdepera was about to be attacked by pirates, the townspeople placed a statue of Our Lady of Hope on the castle walls in sight of the raiders. A fog fell, the terrified pirates fled, and the town was saved. The people of Capdepera still celebrate this each December—*la Fiesta de Nuestra Señora de la Esperanza*.

ARTÀ, eight kilometres from Capdepera, is a quiet rural town surrounded by good hunting country. Here Sunday hunters bag rabbit, hare, partridge and pigeon. Nearly every gate seems to bear a sign proclaiming *Coto Privado de Caza*—private hunting preserve. The 17th-century church (San Salvador) sternly dominates the town. On the outskirts are the Bronze Age ruins of the **Talaiot de Ses Paisses** (see page 10). Archaeologists believe this is one of the oldest continuously inhabited districts of the island, and certainly this is the impression that the spot gives.

## PUERTO DE ALCUDIA
*(Palma, 56 km)*

From Artà to Ca'n Picafort the road eases through gently undulating hills covered with pines. Trees grow in such profusion on Majorca that when Queen Alexandra of England visited the island she said, "One can surely walk from branch to branch across the whole island".

CA'N PICAFORT won't win the "most elegant resort" prize, but it marks the beginning of the island's longest beach—nearly seven miles of white sand stretching as far as Puerto de Alcùdia.

CIUDAD DE LOS LAGOS is a modern resort built from the ground up on reclaimed swamp-land. It is called City of the Lakes because of its location on a network of artificial lakes and canals. Like the Salinas de Levante, this area is a particular favourite with island bird-lovers and ornithologists.

After Ca'n Picafort and Ciudad de los Lagos, PUERTO DE ALCÙDIA comes as a pleasant surprise. It's a slow-paced harbour town, as Majorcan as you can find. Ferries sail from here to the neighbouring island of Minorca. It's blessed with tranquillity but at the same time cursed with mosquitoes which breed in nearby marshes where cotton is grown. The port is an old favourite with Palma families off for the weekend. Hotels and outdoor restaurants line the fishing harbour, and the beaches are good, with water shallow enough for children.

About three kilometres inland is the port's "twin" town of **Alcùdia.** You will want to see the very impressive fortified walls ringing the city, which date from the Middle Ages. You'll notice the 13th-century Church of Santa Ana, one of the oldest in Majorca.

Like many island towns (Pollensa, Andraitx, Sóller), Alcùdia is built several miles inland from the port which served as its trade outlet, the reason being to protect the population from marauding pirates.

Halfway between Alcùdia and its port lay the former Roman capital of the island. The remains of the Roman theatre can still be visited there.

*A stepped path leads up to Artà's 17th-century San Salvador church.*

## PUERTO POLLENSA
*(Palma, 62 km)*

While Alcùdia was the capital of Roman Majorca, it was called *Pollentia*. Somehow during ensuing centuries Pollensa managed to perpetuate the name.

Less than six kilometres from the port of the same name, POLLENSA attracts tourists from nearby resorts who come to climb the famous **Calvari**. This is a flight of 365 cypress-lined steps—one for each day of the year—leading up to a tiny church high above the town. There's also a short, curve-ridden road to the top which passes 14 crosses, marking the Stations of the Cross. From the top the view extends across the crumbling, tiled rooftops of the town to the bays of Pollensa on the left and Alcùdia to the right.

Pollensa—like all Majorcan villages—is dramatically austere. No quaint, flaking whitewash here, but hefty blocks of golden-brown stone that present a totally uniform look. It's a classic island village and fun to explore. Unless your car is not much bigger than a mule, you'd best leave it at the old Plaza Mayor and wander on foot. Pollensa's narrow streets were designed for four-legged, not four-wheeled, traffic.

More impressive views can be had from the ruins of the **Santuari del Puig**, a 14th-century hilltop monastery about a kilometre outside Pollensa. The 980-foot high summit can only be reached on foot, a pleasant hour's stroll

up a narrow, tree-lined path. From the ruins you look out over the countryside with its ploughed fields, olive groves and almond trees.

Each August and September, Majorcan families attack their almond trees with long, wooden poles to knock down the nuts. They collect an estimated 7,000 tons of them annually, two thirds of Spain's total production. Truckloads of almonds go to make *turrón,* the tasty nougat Spaniards are very keen on—especially at village fiestas and during Christmas time.

Tens of thousands of contented holiday-makers claim

*The Mirador de Formentor offers breathtaking vistas of sea and coast.*

*Almonds, knocked by pole from trees, used for turrón (nougat).*

that PUERTO POLLENSA is the prettiest resort town in all Spain. Despite towering hotels and modern villas, the town retains an attractive old-worldliness and an aura of carefree elegance. You can sip drinks beneath the arcades of cafés on the tree-shaded promenade, then cross the road and plunge from white sand into clear water. As a touch of delightful decadence, some hotels have built their swimming pools right on the beach.

Behind the town the hazy silhouette of the nine-mile long **Cabo Formentor** sits stolidly against the horizon. From Pollensa harbour, where sleek international pleasure-craft rub prows with traditional fishing boats, big excursion launches set out to circumnavigate the cape. For stupendous scenery, it's hard to match the drama of the 1,000-foot cliffs thrusting straight from the sea. The voyage ends at CALA DE SAN VICENTE, an up-and-coming resort just a 20-minute drive across the neck of the cape.

Cabo Formentor offers memorable views from land, too. Don't miss the **Mirador de Formentor.** From hundreds of feet above sea-level, you can glimpse Puerto Pollensa, its pretty bay framed by the superb mountains behind you.

Farther along the Mirador road is CALA PI, where the internationally famed Hotel Formentor nestles on the ever-green hillside above its own idyllic beach. This hideaway spot for the rich and titled has been favoured by people like Prince Rainier and Princess Grace of Monaco and the Duke and Duchess of Kent.

# MONASTERY OF LLUCH
*(Palma, 47 km)*

South from Pollensa towards Lluch, the character of the island changes dramatically. Now the road winds up and along the vertebrae of the great mountain chain which is the spine of the island. The sheer spectacle of the ascent illustrates the folly of those who flippantly describe the island as a Palma-on-Sea.

The **Monastery of Lluch,** founded in the 13th century, lies in the bowl of a green, rocky valley, 25 kilometres from Pollensa, 1,300 feet up. It would be hard to find a Majorcan who hasn't visited the site, for this recently restored edifice is a place of pilgrimage for the islanders.

They come to see a bejewelled wooden statue of the Madonna and Child, known affectionately as La Moreneta (the little brown one) because of the colour centuries of aging have given the wood.

Legend claims that the statue was found amongst the rocks by a monk and a shepherd in the 13th century. They took it to a nearby church for safe-keeping. But during the night the statue dis-

*Majorca's popular saint,* La Moreneta, *in Monastery of Lluch.*

appeared. Later it was rediscovered where it had originally been found. Twice more this happened, as though the statue willed that it should not be moved. So a chapel—the foundation for the great monastery which now stands here—was built around the Madonna statue. She immediately captured the popular imagination and became Our Lady of Lluch, the patron saint of Majorca. Each September during the feast day of St. Mary, thousands of Majorcans 49 make a pilgrimage to the site.

The millions of pesetas' worth of jewels which now adorn the statue were donated by the islanders around the end of the last century. The treasure-trove includes 22 diamonds, 25 emeralds, 25 rubies and more than 600 pearls.

Visitors who attend the daily mass at Lluch will be able to hear the internationally famous Lluch boys choir, Els Blavets (the blue boys), who take their name from their distinctive blue cassocks.

The museum displays prehistoric objects, coins, ceramics, religious relics and early Majorcan furniture. The stables look as they did when they were built in 1586. The monastery restaurant serves Majorcan specialities.

A short way from Lluch is the turn-off which winds nearly 12 sinuous kilometres down to the tiny seaside settlement of SA CALOBRA. Here, man-made tunnels which were cut through solid rock in 1950 lead to the mouth of the **Torrents de Pareis** (the twin torrents).

Nicknamed the Grand Canyon of Majorca, this massive ravine was carved by millions of years of winter waters flowing from nearby valleys and emptying into the sea.

Hardy hikers can pack a lunch and explore this two-and-a-half-mile long prehistoric gorge with its 1,000-foot-high walls. The ravine can only be walked in summer and if the torrent is completely dry. The trip can be started from Sa Calobra downstream or upstream from the village of LA ESCORCA, three miles from Lluch, where a path leads into the torrent. Either way it takes four to five hours and at whichever end you finish you're stuck with the problem of finding a ride back.

## PUERTO SOLLER
*(Palma, 35 km)*

The coastal road bends and twists around jagged saw-toothed ridges and rock-strewn slopes. But one short, straight stretch runs through a tunnel and by a dam and reservoir. You'll pass an ancient column, dating from the sixth century B.C., stark and lonely against the wild scenery. "Column of the Sanctuary", a plaque reads, "moved to this place to save it from the waters of the dam, 1969".

Ten more bends, and climbing all the time through the *sierras*, until finally you're through a pass, coasting downhill, and far below are glimpses of a plain. In the middle of it is SÓLLER, surrounded by groves of lemon, orange and almond trees. And behind the village, thrusting its jaw skywards, dominating a spot so lush that the Arabs called it "The Golden Shell", the unmistakable profile of the 4,900-foot-high Puig Mayor, the island's highest mountain.

A similar spectacular scenic trip can be made from Palma to Sóller in the famous *Red Arrow (Flecha Roja)* narrow-gauge train through the Sierra de Alfabia.

PUERTO SÓLLER, five kilometres away, is connected to Sóller by a narrow-gauge tramway and served by a tram said to have been imported from San Francisco early this century. The circular bay is often called the only swimming pool in the world with a town built around it. Quaint and still quiet, though gaining fast in popularity, the port looks French, and not by accident. In previous centuries, communication with the rest of the

*Old-fashioned tram provides rapid service from Sóller down to the sea.*

island depended on precipitous paths cut into the sides of the mountain ranges. So, Sóller and its port turned as much to France for trade and commerce, as to Palma. Surrounded by architecture reminiscent of the south of France, many townspeople even today speak three languages—Majorcan, Castilian and French.

## PUERTO DE ANDRAITX
*(Palma, 35 km)*

The scenery between the Sóller turn-off and Andraitx is the most dramatic on the island: on the left, wooded mountain slopes, broken by terraced fields and olive groves. Some trees, a thousand years old, are twisted into nightmarish caricatures. To the right, more terraces lead to the cliff's brink, the road hugging the absolute edge of the island with sheer drops of hundreds of feet to the ocean below.

DEYÁ, 10 kilometres from Sóller has been a centre for writers and artists ever since Robert Graves, author of *I, Claudius* and *Claudius the God,* adopted it as his permanent home. Once you've seen the village's steep, cobbled streets, charming stone houses and carefully kept gardens, you'll understand why this literary clan calls it home.

Just outside Deyá is **Son Marroig,** a stately old home with grounds stretching to the abrupt coastline. It once was part of the huge Miramar estate of "the man who put Majorca on the map".

He was Archduke Ludwig Salvator of Austria, who first visited the island in 1867 and returned two years later to stay for over 40 years. Having found his island in the sun, he dedicated his life to understanding it. His greatest contribution to island culture was a six-volume study, written in German, called *Die Balearen.* Based on his intimate knowledge of local sociology, geography and botany, the book introduced Majorca to a European public which had been scarcely aware of the island's existence.

The house is open to visitors and filled with mementos relating to the archduke and the Balearics. From the gardens a path leads to a cliff-edge temple which Ludwig Salvator had built from specially imported Carrara marble. You'll enjoy the view of the Toredada, a narrow, rocky promontory lunging out into the sea; the waves have dug a 60-foot-wide hole through it.

The next stop on the round-the-island road, BANYALBUFAR, is a unique village. Over hundreds of years the villagers have tamed the terrain, creating an intricate flight of fertile terraces out of a harsh hillside. Below the village, there's a small beach. Tourists are few, but those who discover the tranquillity and scenic grandeur of Banyalbufar tend to return.

*Because of rocky ground, Spain's cemeteries are often built upwards.*

Between Banyalbufar and the nearby town of Estellencs, the **Torre de las Animas** (tower of the souls) perches on a solid thumb of rock, linked to the mainland's heights by a bridge. The view, hundreds of feet above the sea, is spectacular.

The tower is one of a group ringing the island. They were built after the Reconquest, not only in Majorca but all along Spain's Mediterranean coast, as a measure against pirate attack. If a guard sighted hostile ships, he signalled the next tower, and within a short time the whole island was prepared to defend itself.

The road gradually swings inland for 20 kilometres until a junction lets you head seawards again to SAN TELMO, a relatively unspoiled fishing village. A short, bumpy drive along a dusty road brings you to a hill above Cala Baset. From here you can see the evocative outline of LA DRAGONERA, an approximately four-mile-long offshore island shaped like the back of a dragon emerging from the sea. The island, about two miles from the Majorcan coast, is owned by a Catalonian company which has announced plans to turn it into a playground for the rich.

The town of ANDRAITX, just below the San Telmo junction, all brown stone and straight streets, is dominated by one of Majorca's oldest churches, dating from the early part of the 13th century. Alongside is a cemetery with burial niches ranged four and five high above the ground.

PUERTO DE ANDRAITX, five kilometres downhill, still remains an easy-going fishing town, a favourite of itinerant artists and writers. Though villas and apartments are beginning to sprout on the surrounding slopes, the town keeps its tranquillity and charm. Yachtsmen from all over Europe appreciate the haven of this small harbour in a big, beautiful bay.

From here on, the closer you get to Palma, the livelier the pace. First there's CAMP DE MAR, a popular resort tucked in a pretty cove. Its pine-protected white-sand beach reminds you that the

wild and mountainous west coast is now a long way behind.

After Cala Fornells comes PAGUERA with its extensive beaches and large shopping complex. Then, SANTA PONSA, a modern tourist centre with splendid beaches and water sports. A large cross on the headland marks the place where, on September 10, 1229, King Jaime I landed with his Catalonian army to begin his fight to drive the Moors off Majorca.

*Sentries used to man Torre de las Animas on the lookout for pirates.*

## Two Inland Trips

Most of Majorca's popular attractions are on or near the coast. However, the sights inland merit an excursion, and if you have the time, here are two suggested trips—one on the plain, the other in the highlands. Both start from Palma, but the itineraries are easily adapted to your own location. Either trip could be squeezed into one solid day; two would be better.

### THE PLAIN
*(Es Pla)*

The quickest way out of Palma is by the airport road, which connects with the road to Santanyi. If you're not pressed for time, you can take the beach road through Ca'n Pastilla and El Arenal. Either way, the first large communities are Llucmajor and Campos, country towns surrounded by farmlands and retaining an aura of the 19th century.

LLUCMAJOR, now an important centre for the leather and shoe industries, hasn't seen much excitement since 1349, when King Jaime III was killed here in a battle against his thieving brother-in-law,

Pedro III of Aragón. CAMPOS, on the other hand, was the island hot-spot for contraband in the late 1940s and early 1950s. Fast motor-boats, speeding from African ports, smuggled in cigarettes and soap at the nearby port of Colònia de Sant Jordi. From there the hard-to-get luxury goods were transported to Campos, which was used as a distribution centre for all Majorca.

About four kilometres to the north from Llucmajor and visible for miles around is the

*Harvesting grapes at Felanitx—prospects seem quite promising.*

56

1,800-foot high **Mount Randa,** with a sanctuary tower on its slopes and crowned by a 16th-century monastery.

North-east of Campos, the important agricultural town of FELANITX is famous for its 13th-century, orange-stone church. It's also noted for its cartographers, renowned since the Middle Ages. Majorcans credit them with drawing the maps which set Columbus on his path to the New World in 1492. The local majolica and glass industry have plenty of adepts... not to mention the white wine.

Felanitx is the base for two side-trips, both to hilltops.

The first goes to the ruins of **Santueri Castle.** Dating from the Roman occupation and then continually added to during the Middle Ages, it completely dominates the surrounding plain. On a clear day, from the walls of the outer keep you can see as far as the island of Cabrera, 25 miles away.

Close by, on the summit of the 1,670-foot-high **Puig de San Salvador,** is the 13th-century Sanctuary of Our Saviour (San Salvador). Next to the church you'll see a small

*The 13th-century church at Felanitx is a must for visitors to the town.*

room full of hundreds of votive offerings, some a century old, from ill and injured people who prayed here for help.

MANACOR, traditionally a centre for crafts and craftsmen, remains so today with olive-wood carpentry shops, furniture factories, ceramic shops and artificial-pearl factories. With a population of over 24,000, it's also the island's second largest city though less than a tenth the size of Palma.

Majorca's artificial pearls are world famous. The best are made from a nucleus with the same specific weight as the real pearl, coated with exact colourings compounded from fish-scales and so scientifically made that not even experts can tell the difference until they feel the smoothness of the artificial pearl compared with the distinctive roughness of the real thing. Several pearl factories offer organized tours and demonstrate the complete process.

From Manacor a 12-kilometre drive leads to Porto Cristo and the caves of Drach or Hams (see page 41). The village of PETRA is in the other direction.

In 1713, this ancient farming village with its brown stone houses was the birthplace of Junípero Serra, Majorca's famous missionary. The Franciscan friar travelled to the Americas and founded the settlements which eventually blossomed into California's great cities–Los Angeles, San Francisco, San Diego and San Jose.

Today you can visit the house where Serra was born, which has been preserved with furniture and utensils dating from his era. An old wine cellar beside the house contains a collection of 18th- and 19th-century farm implements. In the same street is a museum documenting the life of the missionary. His statue stands in a palm-shaded square near a street named Calle California.

From Petra you can go either directly back to Palma, or take the longer road to the heart of the island and the town of INCA. Here you can visit a leather factory and see Santa María la Mayor, a church begun in the 13th century. While you're here, you may want to sample some specialities of Inca—roast sucking pig and lamb—served in one of the town's wine-cellar restaurants, renowned throughout the Balearics.

From Inca the road back to Palma cuts through the vineyards of BINISSALEM, headquarters of Majorca's wine industry. In the town of SANTA MARÍA you can visit the ancient Convento de Mínimos now housing a Majorcan museum, and a church with a painting on gold of the Madonna, dating from the 14th century.

## THE HIGHLANDS
### (Sa Muntanya)

Twenty kilometres from Palma, at VALLDEMOSSA, the former Carthusian monastery called **La Cartuja** was the home, during the bleak winter of 1838, of the scandal-prone French authoress George Sand and her Polish lover, Frédéric Chopin.

Three years earlier, the monks who had lived and worked here were ousted by

*Chopin composed* Raindrop Prelude *during a winter stay at La Cartuja.*

political decree, and the cells of the monastery were publicly auctioned and converted into apartments.

The winter spent at Valldemossa was not a happy one for the two lovers. In her book, *A Winter in Majorca,* Sand describes her neighbours as "barbarians, thieves and monkeys" and likens them to Polynesian savages. But here Chopin produced some of his finest compositions. Today throngs of music-lovers and others visit the monastery's cell No. 2 where the couple lived.

The all-in ticket for La Cartuja includes the monks' pharmacy, the prior's cell with its magnificent library and the adjacent Palace of King Sancho.

Ten kilometres south, and close by the village of Esporlas, is the privately owned **La Granja** estate. The manorial farmhouse with its surrounding property has been turned into a "living" museum of rural Majorcan life, where time-honoured handicrafts are preserved. Here, workers wearing traditional costumes demonstrate aspects of island farmlife as it was before mechanization. They make lace and pottery, plait dried grass into harnesses and mats, forge iron tools, weave cloth and carpets, spin cotton and churn butter. Included in the ticket price are donkey rides, snacks and wine, folk-dancing and other entertainment.

*At La Granja, as all over Spain, youngsters keep old crafts alive.*

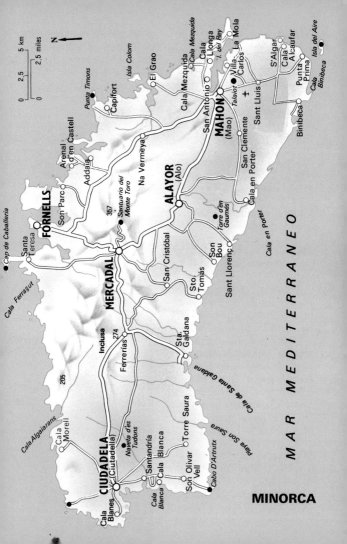

**Minorca**

Any good travel agent will suggest that you only take a long holiday on Minorca if you are seeking absolute peace and quiet. These are Minorca's unique and priceless commodities.

Majorca may be everyone's idea of holiday paradise. Ibiza may boast of its "beautiful people". But Minorca—the tranquil island of the western Mediterranean—just slumbers on. It is host to fewer than 250,000 visitors a year, less than 10 per cent of Majorca's visitors.

Minorca can be reached by plane from Barcelona and Palma and by ferry from Barcelona, Palma and Alcùdia.

It was named Minorca ("the smaller") by the Romans who needed some simple way to distinguish it from Majorca ("the larger"), about 25 miles away. On an area of 30 miles by 12, it has a population of about 50,000.

If you're visiting from Majorca, one day will give you a mere glimpse of what this island has to offer. Allow yourself two, or better, three days, and you'll have time for a leisurely look. Better still, a week or two will give you a chance to enjoy to the full the island's fresh air, pleasant countryside and long, clean beaches, some of which are near-deserted.

The two major cities, Mahón and Ciudadela, are 45 kilometres apart at opposite ends of the island and connected by a good road.

## MAHON (MAO)
Pop. 25,000

The capital of the island is a strait-laced and slightly dour little city. Its four-mile-long harbour is considered the finest deep-water anchorage in the world apart from Pearl Harbour. In the 1700s this geographical treasure put a gleam in the eye of every power with ambitions in the Mediterranean and made Port Mahón a bone of contention for a century.

The British took the island in 1708 during the War of the

*Sunset over Mahón harbour, one of the world's finest natural anchorages.*

Spanish Succession and their occupation was ratified by the Treaty of Utrecht in 1713. The French grabbed it in 1756 during the Seven Years' War; the Treaty of Paris returned it to Britain in 1763. Then, in 1781, a combined Spanish-French expedition succeeded in occupying the island, and the Spanish flag flew again. Slightly soured, the British took a breather and didn't attempt to retake it until 1798. In 1802 the Treaty of Amiens returned the island to Spain once and for all. The Minorcans—who for a hundred years must have felt like the first prize in an international lottery—returned to their farms and fishing boats.

But the French and British occupations have left their mark on Mahón. Wandering through the city today you find more than a hint of England in the Georgian architecture and the sash-windows (said to be found nowhere else in Spain). The local Catalan dialect, Menorquín, which is closely related to the language spoken on Majorca, contains many words absorbed from both French and English.

More palatable survivors from the occupation are gin and mayonnaise. Distilleries in Mahón still produce gin following British recipes introduced during the 18th century. Some brands are bottled in old-fashioned pottery containers and connoisseurs insist that the product is better than that made in England.

Mayonnaise, or perhaps more correctly "mahonnaise", is claimed, by the Minorcans at least, to have been invented in Mahón. The story goes that in 1756 the Duke of Richelieu went to a backstreet inn in Mahón and ordered dinner. The inn-keeper had nothing but some leftover meat, so he cunningly disguised it with a sauce which delighted the duke so much he promptly dubbed it *la salsa mahonesa,* Mahón sauce.

Mahón was once encircled by walls to protect it from seaborne invasion. A reminder of those days, a 16th-century arch, straddles Carrer Sant Roc.

In the **Casa de la Cultura,** an archaeological museum has been created around such diverse objects as Phoenician relics and Aztec sculpture brought from the New World.

You can stroll down to the docks via the steep flight of steps which crosses the Calle

## BERLITZ® GOES VIDEO – *FOR LANGUAGES*

Here's a brand new 90-minute video from Berlitz for learning key words and phrases for your trip. It's easy and fun. Berlitz language video combines computer graphics with live action and freeze frames. You see on your own TV screen the type of dialogue you will encounter abroad. You practice conversation by responding to questions put to you in the privacy of your own living room.

Shot on location for accuracy and realism, Berlitz gently leads you through travel situations towards language proficiency. Available from video stores and selected bookstores and Berlitz Language Centers everywhere. Only $59.95 plus $3.00 for shipping and handling.

To order by credit card, call 1-800-228-2028 Ext. 35.
Coming soon to the U.K.

Abundancia. But if you have the time, take a launch trip around the bay, an excursion advertised in many hotels.

Two of the harbour's three islands once served as quarantine stations. The smaller was leased to the United States Navy in the 19th century and was used as a training base for midshipmen until the opening of the Naval Academy at Annapolis, Maryland.

On the Cala Llonga side of the harbour, the 250-foot-high La Mola Peninsula, a natural defence position, at one time bristled with cannons. The modern gun emplacements are part of a Spanish military post.

Closer to Mahón, high on the hills on the north side of the harbour, palm trees surround an imposing old, pink-coloured mansion. It's built in the Georgian style—with distinct Spanish touches—and although named the Villa San Antonio, it's better known as the Golden Farm.

Lord Nelson is said to have stayed in the house while his fleet was anchored in Mahón

*Off the beaten track, many unspoilt beaches like this one can be found.*

*Walls of stone and of pumpkins symbolize division of Minorca.*

harbour. But legends are sometimes more interesting than facts: no records prove that Nelson ever set foot on Minorcan soil, and the present owners of the Golden Farm only smile when you mention the story.

On the **Villa Carlos** side (the old Georgetown of British

days) stands the 16th-century San Felipe Fort. The inlet which separates the fort and the star-shaped Marlborough redoubt is visible from outside the harbour. Local legend claims that the two are connected by a tunnel dug beneath the inlet.

In the south-eastern corner of the island below Mahón, a string of beach resorts is being developed. The most interesting is BINIBECA, a very recent holiday centre built in the style of a fishing village. Sprouting up the side of the cove like an architect's surrealistic dream, it's Minorca's swinging showpiece.

## ACROSS THE ISLAND

Minorca is divided into two distinct geographical zones. North of the Mahón-Ciudadela road is lush, undulating farmland—almost northern European–with blackberry bushes lining the road and cows grazing in the greenest fields to be found in all the Balearics. The cows are the mainstay of the island's flourishing cheese industry. Mahón cheese *(queso de Mahón)* is one of the best-known in Spain.

*Monumental prehistoric* taula *easily dwarfs today's awestruck visitors.*

South of the road, this island is a rock-strewn wilderness. The tough Minorcans have spent generations trying to clear the land, and the results of their back-breaking work are found in mile after mile of neatly built stone walls. At times, especially in narrow back lanes, the walls are so close together that it's like driving through a tunnel.

Perhaps it was this abundance of building materials which prompted Minorca's Bronze Age population to construct what are now the island's most fascinating attractions. More than 500 prehistoric sites have been found on Minorca, nearly all of them to the south of the Ciudadela road. Archaeologists consider it an outdoor museum.

Apart from commonplace prehistoric dwellings, architectural forms exist on Minorca which are found nowhere else in the world except in Majorca and Sardinia. They are the *taula,* the *naveta* and the *talaiot.*

The *taula* is a massive *T* made from two huge blocks of stone. The upright may be as high as 16 feet and the crossbar 10 feet long. The purpose of the *taula* is unknown, though it's presumed to have held some religious significance. How a pre-mechanical civilization was able to place such enormous stone blocks into position is still an enigma. 67

The *taula* at **Trebalugar,** just behind the village of Villa Carlos, is relatively easy to reach.

The *naveta,* a vaguely ship-shaped building, may have been used as a burial chamber. About five kilometres from Ciudadela you'll find the **Naveta d'es Tudons.** Restored in 1952, it is one of the oldest man-made structures in Europe.

The *talaiot* is a tower-like structure, between 20 and 40 feet high, with an inner chamber. Its function still remains a total mystery (see page 10).

To see a *talaiot,* go to **Torre d'en Gaumes,** south of Alayor, the largest prehistoric settlement on the island—half a square mile of rubble to some, absolute fascination to others.

Searching for prehistoric remains introduces you to one of the most interesting—and frustrating—experiences. As the paved road ends, so do the road signs. Sometimes, with luck, you'll find an old sign tacked to a building at a cross-roads telling you which way to turn, but at the next cross-roads you'll just have to

*Binibeca: a refreshing departure from the usual resort architecture.*

guess. Then, after bounding along a dusty, pot-holed road, you might see a farmer. If so, ask him for directions.

When at last you've reached the monument you've been hunting for, the chances are it will be on private land. If you see a sign on the gate, it will probably mean "please shut the gate".

The main road between Mahón and Ciudadela runs part of the way beside a secondary road originally built by order of Sir Richard Kane, the island's first British governor (1713–25).

On the route to Ciudadela is ALAYOR (ALÓ) famed for its shoe-making (hand-made shoes from Minorca are exported all over Europe) as well as for its Italian-style ice-cream.

On the last bends in the road down to popular PLAYA DE SON BOU are man-made caves, hacked out of the steep face of the cliff thousands of years ago. (The Cala en Porter and Cala Coves area of Minorca contain 140 more caves. To the delight of holiday-makers, some have been turned into discotheques and cafés.) Son Bou also is the site of a 5th- or 6th-century Christian basilica discovered in 1951.

SANTA GALDANA is a classic Balearic cove: a huge horseshoe of white sand backed by the greenest of pines. The resort occupies an idyllic site, but its tranquillity is a thing of the past. New apartment blocks and hotels cater to a growing influx of visitors.

The picturesque fishing village of **Fornells,** in the middle of the north coast, has a huge bay all to itself. While you're here, you ought to try one of the sea-food restaurants, where lobster is a speciality.

*Individualist in a fast-declining industry: fisherman at Fornells.*

Like most Minorcan villages, it is gleaming white in surprising contrast to the sombre brown of the towns on neighbouring Majorca; some families even paint their roofs white.

Nearby are the ruins of a Phoenician village.

If you want a beach to yourself, head for the nearly deserted northwestern corner of the island. You may have to explore on foot, but the chance of finding a secluded slice of paradise makes it worth the effort.

*Children of all nationalities mix easily at play in the Balearics.*

### CIUDADELA (CIUTADELLA)
Pop. 18,000

Ciudadela, on the island's west coast, was once the capital of Minorca. But its beautiful harbour could not match the importance of Mahón's in size and strategic value. So, during Kane's governorship, the seat of power was moved to the other side of the island. Ciudadela, however, remains the island's ecclesiastical capital.

This ancient town, which may have been founded by the Phoenicians, is so different from Mahón that it's hard to believe both cities belong on the same small island. While Mahón is business-minded, sedate and in debt to foreign influence, Ciudadela is happy, bright and exuberantly Spanish. Business seems very much a peripheral activity.

Meander through the old white-washed back streets to the quaint Sa Plaça Nova. The street leading from the plaza to the 14th-century Gothic cathedral, **Ses Arcades**, is the loveliest street on the island—it's all archways and completely Moorish in character.

The square called **Es Born** is the hub of the town. The

town hall (*Ayuntamiento*), facing the square, was once the home of the Moorish governors. A portrait of Adm. David Farragut, the American Civil War naval hero, hanging inside will probably surprise most Americans. Farragut's father was born on the island and later emigrated to the United States.

When you begin to tire, make your way to Plaza de Alfonso III. Here at the old Café Es Molí, topped by a windmill tower, you can take a glass of chilled white wine and just relax.

*The picturesque harbour at Ciudadela, formerly the island's capital.*

# What to Do

## The Bullfight

If you've never seen a bull-fight, a holiday on Majorca may be just the opportunity to witness Spain's most popular national attraction. You may be repelled by parts of the spectacle, or you may become a lifelong aficionado. But whatever your reaction, you'll recognize that the *corrida* is a unique experience.

The bull has been bred to fight in the ring, and the matador has devoted his life towards finalizing the ritual. His own death—though always a very real possibility—has no place in the proceedings.

The fight is divided into *tercios* (thirds), each designed to tire the bull. First the bull comes into the ring and helpers play it with capes so that the matador can study the way it moves, the way it prefers to thrust with its horns. Then the matador takes over and tries the bull himself, using the big red and yellow *capote*. This is perhaps the most beautiful part of the fight. But beautiful as it may be, every single movement by the matador is calculated to bring the bull closer to the inevitable finale.

The first *tercio* begins when the *picador,* the mounted spearman, uses his lance on the bull's huge shoulder muscles. This spearing has two purposes: it tires the bull, and it forces him to drop his head into a position which will allow the matador to place his sword. The audience invariably boos the *picador,* not for any love of the bull, but simply because if the spear is used too much, the bull will lose his strength and his will to fight. After the *picador, banderilleros* place darts in the bull's shoulders during the second *tercio* to counter any preference the animal may have for hooking with either horn.

Finally comes the last *tercio* when the matador fights the bull with the small, dark red *muleta.* Gradually he dominates the bull—even to the point where he can turn his back on it and walk away. At last the climax is reached: a time which has come to be known in English as "the moment of truth". With the bull theoretically completely under his control, the matador

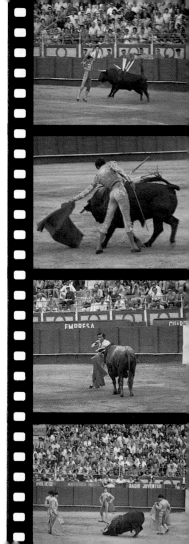

sights along his sword and then lunges, leaning dangerously over the bull's horns to thrust the weapon into a minute area between the shoulder blades which should kill the bull within seconds. Depending upon the quality and bravery of the performance, the fight's *el presidente* will indicate whether or not the matador is to be awarded an ear, two ears or, after an exceptional performance, the tail of the animal he has killed.

You may be sickened, fascinated or simply confused. Most foreigners are. But you will have witnessed a violent act which at times contains incredible beauty. With luck you will come to understand why this unforgettable ballet of death is considered an art form.

Majorca's main bullring (*Plaza de Toros*) is in Palma, where matadors fight during the summer. Fights are also held in the ring at Inca and occasionally in nearby Muro.

Among several seating categories at the bullring, the best may be *sol y sombra,* which means that you'll be in sun for part of the fight, shade for the rest. It is a good compromise between the expense of sombra and the heat in the *sol.*

For a small fee you can have your name along with the greatest!

## Flamenco

Flamenco music and dancing were born in Andalusia, and the region remains the stronghold of the art. However, you'll be able to visit a *tablao*—a floor show featuring guitarists, singers and dancers—during your island holiday. Flamenco is said to have Moorish origins; you may find it has a striking resemblance to the wailing chants so typical of Arab music.

There are two main groups of flamenco songs. One, the bouncier and more cheerful, is known as the *cante chico* (the light song). *Fandangos, sevillanas, bulerías, alegrías, mala-*

*gueñas* are all part of the *cante chico.*

The themes of the cante chico are light, but sometimes they can be touching. One *sevillana* records a conversation between the Rose and the Snow. The Rose pleads that the sun come out lest she die. The Snow replies that the Rose has no pity, because with the sun he'll perish, and he wants to be with her a little longer. At the end of the song, the Rose is found dead in the middle of a puddle.

The second group of songs is the *cante jondo* (the song of the soul). Slow, piercing and nearly always brutally emotional, it deals with the intricacies of love, death and the human predicament. It is the style of the great flamenco singers.

But it is the *cante chico* you'll hear at the *tablao flamenco.* These shows, which usually include a drink and a certain amount of audience participation, are staged in many tourist resorts.

## Traditional Dances

As living standards rise and the pace of life quickens, folklore tends to fade from the

*Excitement, poetry and elegance blend in Spanish flamenco dance.*

front rank of island interests. It's feared that in another generation or so Majorca's native dances will only be memories. But for the moment you still have the chance to enjoy authentic, living folklore.

The island's oldest dance, *els cossiers,* is performed in country towns at fiestas. Another dance, the *parado,* resembles an old court minuet. It's typical of Valldemossa, where you can see it performed in the square of King Sancho's Palace beside the monastery.

A regional dance from Binissalem, the *tal de vermadors,* tells the story of a group of brave women defending their homes against invaders. It is 75 performed in simple, working clothes, but most folk dances require elaborate finery. Costumes and the typical music and steps are demonstrated at the La Granja estate near Esporlas (see page 60).

One of Minorca's distinctive dances, the *ball d'es cossil,* may have its origins in Scottish highland dance. Another, performed during fiesta time in the village of San Cristóbal is reminiscent of the English maypole dance. Both traditions are supposed to have been introduced during the English occupation.

*Traditional folk dances and costumes can be seen at many village fiestas.*

# Shopping

## Shopping Hours

Most Majorcan stores are open from 9 a.m. to 1.30 p.m. and again from 4.30 or 5 to 8 p.m. The hours in between are devoted to lunch and that most venerable of Spanish customs, the siesta. In summer, shops in tourist resorts often stay open until 10 p.m. Bars and cafés are generally open from about 8 a.m. to midnight or later.

## Best Buys

Majorca is famous for its leather and suède clothing, footwear, artificial pearls and glassware.

Most leather and suède comes from Inca, where you can visit a factory and then choose an item from the showroom.

Even though so-called factory prices are not much lower than those you'll find in Palma, the product ought to cost significantly less than on the mainland or in your home country.

Majorcan artificial pearls are exported all over the world and are exceptional value for the money. Manacor is the town to visit if you want to join a tour round a pearl factory and adjacent showrooms which display a complete range of the finished product (see page 58).

There are several glass factories on the island where you are welcome to watch artisans at work fashioning exotic shapes by blowing molten glass attached to long, hollow metal rods.

Probably the best buy in Majorca today—as in the rest of Spain—is footwear. Shoes and boots, both men's and women's, can be quite cheap and of good quality. However, children's shoes tend to be more expensive than in the rest of Europe. Both Majorca and Minorca produce footwear for the home and international markets. (Most Parisian makes of shoe are manufactured in Majorca and Minorca.)

While you window-shop around Palma or Mahón you may be struck by the high quality of children's clothing and by their unexpectedly high prices. Jewellery (bisutería) is a Minorcan speciality: hunt around.

Liquor and cigarettes are remarkably cheap by Euro- 77

pean and American standards. Top foreign-brand drinks produced under licence in Spain are a real bargain, despite recent price hikes, and Spanish-made cigarettes are even better value. A selection of imported Cuban cigars is available at prices much lower than you would pay almost anywhere in Europe.

Locally produced pottery, colourful and useful, is usually quite cheap. Most tourist resorts have at least one pottery shop. Several resorts are visited by salesmen leading donkeys laden with jugs and vases. You can try your hand at haggling with these vendors.

## Souvenirs

You'll find plenty of "traditional" Spanish souvenirs on the islands: bullfight posters (with or without your own name printed on them), bullfighter swords, inlaid Arab-style chess-sets, a wide selection of swords and pistols produced in Toledo, wrought

*Souvenirs of every description abound. Wise shoppers compare prices.*

ironwork and the typical Spanish *bota,* a wineskin. (If you buy a *bota,* make sure it isn't lined with plastic.)

Other items—produced as much for local consumption as for the tourist trade—are hand-made shawls, embroidered linen, lace-work, painted fans and hand-woven shopping baskets.

An unusual type of souvenir, available in Majorca and nowhere else in Spain, is the *siurell,* a comical looking hand-painted clay figure which has existed on the island in one form or another since the days of the Phoenicians. The significance of the form has long been forgotten, but a *siurell,* which comes with a built-in whistle, makes an amusing and unusual decorative piece.

Full-colour postcards are still the cheapest in Europe.

### Antiques

If you know what you're looking for, you'll find worthwhile antiques in Spain. By now, Majorca has been well raked over, but a few good pieces are still around. Palma has several antique shops. The outdoor flea market held on Saturday mornings around Gabriel Alomar i Villalonga is worth a close look as well.

You're most likely to find old keys, iron-work, hand-carved wooden bowls, brightly painted tiles and paintings and prints.

### Where to shop

Tourist centres on the island may look like shopping paradises, but they are frequently tourist traps. All too often the shops offer inferior quality items. They rarely have a full

*...and remember that in outdoor markets prices are negotiable.*

selection, and their prices tend to be higher.

It's best to save your important shopping for the island capitals of Palma and Mahón. You're likely to save up to 20 per cent on your purchases.

## Shopping Tips

Wherever you decide to do your shopping, but particularly in the resort towns, it's worth comparing prices in several shops before making your decision. Plenty of shops simply overcharge.

You can ask for a discount in a big shop, but bargaining is out. Save that for the antique shops and outdoor markets.

The Spanish government levies a value added tax (called "IVA") on most items. Tourists from abroad will be refunded the IVA they pay on purchases over a stipulated amount. To obtain the rebate, you have to fill out a form, provided by the shops. The shop keeps one copy; the three others must be presented at the customs on departure, together with the goods. The rebate will then be forwarded by the shop to your home address.

## FIESTAS AND FESTIVALS

Spain is the land of *fiesta,* and the Balearics have their share of both religious and folk festivals. The dates of some vary from year to year. Here are the highlights for Majorca and Minorca:

**Procession of the Magi,** Palma, January 5. The Magi, or the Three Kings, are the Spanish version of Santa Claus. This is when the children receive their Christmas gifts. You can watch the kings ferried across Palma Bay under a rain of fireworks and then follow their parade through the centre of the island capital.

**Holy Week processions,** Palma, Holy Week. A great spectacle, with hundreds of men carrying holy images through the streets to the sound of muffled drums.

**Moors and Christians,** Sóller, in May; Pollensa, in August. Part of the celebration of the Feast of Our Lady of Victory is a vivid re-enactment of the reconquest of the island. "Moors" and "Christians" fight a mock battle.

*From baby-bullfights to pole climbs, it's all here at Cortijo Vista Verde.*

80

**Feast of St. John,** Ciudadela, June 24. Minorca's most important *fiesta,* it includes a jousting tournament with horsemen in traditional costume trying to spear small rings. Then they dash through the streets while citizens pelt them with hazelnuts.

**Feast of St. Lawrence,** Alayor, August 10. Typical Minorcan festival, the climax *(es jaleo)* of which is reached when horsemen enter the crowded main square and make their horses stand up on their hind feet.

**Wine Festival,** Binissalem, in October. Wine and folklore.

**Dijous Bo** (literally, "Good Thursday"), Inca, in November. Majorca's biggest agricultural fair. Includes folkloric events.

## MUSEUMS AND GALLERIES

Here's a selection of Majorca's and Minorca's museums and art galleries you'll find worthwhile visiting:

**Museum of Archaeology and Fine Arts** *(Museo Arqueológico y de Bellas Artes),* Plaza Conquista, 8, Mahón. Historical records, prehistoric exhibits and paintings.

**Bellver Castle** *(Museo Municipal),* Palma. Objects relating to island history.

**Cathedral Museum** *(Museo de la Catedral)* or Cathedral Treasury *(Tesoro de la Catedral).* Collection of tapestries, paintings, altar ornaments and religious relics, including a splinter said to have come from the True Cross.

**Diocesan Museum** *(Museo Arqueológico Diocesano)* in the Episcopal Palace, Calle del Palau, Palma. Icons, ceramics, coins and paintings depicting the island's history.

**Vivot Palace** *(Palacio Vivot),* Calle Zavella, 2, Palma. Medieval tapestries, books and furnishings in an old Majorcan palace. (Only open when the family is in residence.)

**Art Mansion** *(Mansión de Arte)* at Calle Apuntadores, 45, Palma. Works mainly by Spanish artists (Ribera, Morales).

**Krekovic Museum** *(Museo Krekovic)* at Calle de Ciudad de Querétaro, Palma. A unique collection of paintings relating to the ancient Inca empire.

## FILMS

Almost all films are dubbed in Spanish but there are cinemas in Magaluf, Palma and El Terreno which occasionally show films in their original version.

## CASINO

The Casino Sporting Club Mallorca, open from 8 p.m. to 4 a.m. daily, offers American and French roulette, blackjack, etc., and has a restaurant-theatre.

## BARBECUES

Several barbecue establishments operate in Majorca. Open on a year-round basis are those of Son Amar in the Palma area, Es Moli d'es Comte near Establiments, Ses Rotes near Esporlas, Son Termens and Comte Mal which also has jousting.

## MARINELAND

At Palma Nova, trained dolphins and sea-lions perform in a pool-stadium.

## BABY BULLS

At the Cortijo Vista Verde in Ca'n Pastilla, tourists have a chance to fight baby bulls (with no danger to the bulls). Later, there's a flamenco show with free "champagne".

## SAFARI PARK

Just north of Porto Cristo, you can drive your car on a 2½ mile circuit through the park of 100 acres, or join a group on a safari. Rhinos, elephants and giraffes, among other beasts. There's also a zoo of smaller, caged animals from Africa.

# Wining and Dining

1 *Manchego cheese* (queso manchego); 2 *Rioja wine* (vino de Rioja); 3 *sherry* (vino de Jerez); 4 *prawns* (gambas); 5 *sardines* (sardinas); 6 *squid* (calamar); 7 *whitebait* (chanquetes); 8 *grapes* (uvas); 9 *clam* (almeja); 10 *sea bream* (besugo); 11 *green peppers* (pimientos); 12 *Spanish omelet* (tortilla española); 13 *salad* (ensalada); 14 *chilled vegetable soup* (gazpacho)

"In the south they fry", goes the Spanish saying, "in the centre they roast, and in the north they stew". In the islands they do all three, so you can look forward to some varied and memorable treats.

In many tourist hotels the food tends to be a bland, inter-national compromise: your pleasure will be as limited as the chef's inspiration. The an-swer is to eat out and to track down the restaurants and dishes favoured by the Ma-jorcans and Minorcans themselves.

But being isolated from

mainland Spain, the Balearics have specialities of their own. Here are some Majorcan dishes worth trying:

*Lechona:* Roast sucking-pig is the island's greatest culinary triumph. Available in most Majorcan restaurants, you'll probably taste it at its best in one of the old converted "wine-cellar restaurants" in Inca.

*Sopa Mallorquina:* Something between a soup and a stew, it's prepared from the simplest of ingredients: bread, green vegetables (cauliflower when in season), garlic and onions.

*Frito Mallorquín:* A combination of fried liver, kidneys, green peppers, potatoes and leeks. It may not sound appetizing, but it's surprisingly delicious.

*Tumbet:* Aubergines, peppers, potatoes and tomatoes fried in olive oil.

*Sobrasada:* Pork-liver sausage.

*Pa amb oli:* Majorcan version of the open sandwich. Country bread spread with oil and topped with fresh tomato and slices of mountain ham.

*Caracoles:* Snails, served with a garlic mayonnaise sauce.

## Seafood

On a Mediterranean island it would be a shame not to sample the fish, and here are some you may want to try. They are usually fried or grilled and then served without sauce, though often with a tomato, onion and lettuce salad offered as an optional side-dish:

*Calamares*—squid
*Gambas*—prawns (shrimp)
*Langosta*—spiny lobster (when in season; always expensive)
*Lenguado*—sole
*Mero*—sea bass
*Salmonetes*—Mediterranean red mullet

*Tapas:* These are tasty, bite-sized morsels of such varied foods as roast meat, meatballs, olives, fried fish, shellfish, vegetable salad, etc. The word *tapa* means "lid", and the term comes from the old custom of giving a bite of food with a drink, the food being served on a tiny plate which covered the glass. These days, sadly, the old custom of giv- 85 ing *tapas* is dying, but the idea of selling them is stronger than ever. Some bars specialize in *tapas,* where, instead of sitting down to a formal meal, you can spend hours sipping wine and eating your way down a long bar crammed with tastily prepared dishes.

Two classic Spanish dishes, as popular in the islands as they are on the mainland, are *paella* and *gazpacho. Gazpacho* is a chilled vegetable soup of green peppers, cucumbers, onions, croutons, oil, vinegar and spices—many of which are served on the side and may be added according to taste. It's been described as "liquid salad" and makes an ideal first course to a fish dinner. *Paella,* the best-known of all Spanish dishes, usually combines seafood and chicken, pork or rabbit, served on a bed of saffron-flavoured rice. Normally served at lunchtime, the best *paellas* are always cooked to order and take at least half an hour to prepare.

### Breakfast

In Spain breakfast is the least important meal of the day. It's usually just a cup of coffee and a crescent roll or doughnut. For a Balearic-type breakfast, try an *ensaimada,* a light, round, flaky bun made from dough and lard and sprinkled with icing sugar. They are so popular that tourists now buy them specially packed to take back home.

In deference to foreign habits most hotels and some cafés now serve a *desayuno completo,* a breakfast usually including coffee, butter, jam or marmalade and rolls or toast.

### Restaurants

Spanish restaurants are officially graded by forks, from one to five, the latter being the most elegant. But forks are awarded according to facilities available and the size of the menu, neither of which has anything to do with the quality of the food.

Spanish restaurants usually offer a *menú del día* (menu of the day or set menu). For a fixed price you'll get three courses plus wine. The price depends on the rating of the restaurant. Most fixed-price and à-la-carte menus include service, but in Spain it is customary to leave a tip. Ten per cent would be normal, 15 per cent generous.

Most restaurants are open for lunch from 1 to 3 p.m. Dinner is normally served from 8 until 10 p.m.

One hint for keeping costs down is to order the *vino de la casa* (house wine). It will cost you only a half or two-thirds the price of a bottled wine.

**Bars and Cafés**
These establishments are an important institution in Spanish life. Some open at first light to cater for early morning workers; nearly all are open by 8.30 a.m. to serve breakfast. Open-air cafés are justifiably popular with tourists.

*There's no need to rush your drink at Majorca's sunny outdoor cafés.*

*However cramped the table space, the conviviality knows no bounds.*

One of the great pleasures of the Mediterranean is to sit outside in the early morning with a *café con leche* (white coffee) and watch a town come to life. The price of a coffee buys you a seat at a table for as long as you care to sit there.

While in a café or bar you might be approached by lottery-ticket vendors, flower-sellers and bootblacks. If you don't want what they offer, simply say *no, gracias.*

Wines and spirits are served at all hours in bars and cafés. Bills include service, but small tips are the custom. It's usually 10–15 per cent cheaper to take a coffee or a drink at the bar rather than sitting at a table.

## Wines and Spirits

The most famous of all Spanish wines is sherry *(jerez),* which comes from the Andalusian town of Jerez de la Frontera. There are two main types: *fino* and *oloroso.* As an aperitif, try a *fino (manzanillas* and *amontillados*—dry, pale and with a rich bouquet—are *finos).* An *oloroso* (brown and cream sherries—heavier and darker—but also the pale, medium-dry *amoroso*) makes a good and somewhat different after-dinner drink, satisfying but not sickly. Sherry wine is fortified with the addition of brandy.

Table wines are quite adequate, and some can be excellent. Among the cheaper wines, try those from Valdepeñas; for higher quality wines, those from Rioja. Don't fail to sample the red wine produced on Majorca itself.

The Spanish type of champagne is often very sweet. You might get something more to your taste by asking for a semi-dry *(semi-seco)* or a dry *(seco).*

Spanish brandy (also produced in Jerez) can be very good, but be sure to ask for one of the better brands. Ordering a cheap brandy may leave you with an unjustly bad impression of the Spanish product.

Spain is a bonanza for liquor and liqueur drinkers. Most drinks are made under licence in the country and cost about half what you pay in most European countries. Imported Scotch is a major exception.

Majorca produces three liqueurs of its own: *hierbas seca, hierbas dulce* and *palo*. *Hierbas seca* ("dry herbs") and *hierbas dulce* ("sweet herbs") are aniseed drinks like the mainland *anís* but bottled with herbs to produce a special flavour. For the best *hierbas* look in the mountainous north-west of the island. There you can drink the home-made variety, much superior to the commercial product. *Palo* is a liqueur made from crushed carob seeds, very sweet, very sticky and usually laced with gin. In Minorca, locally distilled gin follows recipes introduced by the British when they were in control of the island.

*Sangría* is an extremely popular summer drink. It's a cooling mixture of red wine, brandy, mineral water, orange and lemon juices to which sliced fruit is added. Spaniards drink it as a refresher. Tourists who take it with their meals may find it too heavy and strong.

## TO HELP YOU ORDER...

Could we have a table? **¿Nos puede dar una mesa?**
Do you have a set menu? **¿Tiene un menú del día?**
I'd like a/an/some... **Quisiera...**

| | | | |
|---|---|---|---|
| beer | **una cerveza** | milk | **leche** |
| bread | **pan** | mineral water | **agua mineral** |
| coffee | **un café** | napkin | **una servilleta** |
| condiments | **los condimentos** | potatoes | **patatas** |
| cutlery | **los cubiertos** | rice | **arroz** |
| dessert | **un postre** | salad | **una ensalada** |
| fish | **pescado** | sandwich | **un bocadillo** |
| fruit | **fruta** | soup | **una sopa** |
| glass | **un vaso** | sugar | **azúcar** |
| ice-cream | **un helado** | tea | **un té** |
| meat | **carne** | (iced) water | **agua (fresca)** |
| menu | **la carta** | wine | **vino** |

# ...AND READ THE MENU

| | | | |
|---|---|---|---|
| aceitunas | olives | guisantes | peas |
| ajo | garlic | helado | ice-cream |
| albaricoques | apricots | higos | figs |
| albóndigas | meatballs | huevos | eggs |
| almejas | baby clams | jamón | ham |
| anchoas | anchovies | judías | beans |
| anguila | eel | langosta | spiny lobster |
| arroz | rice | langostino | prawn |
| asado | roast | lenguado | sole |
| atún | tunny (tuna) | limón | lemon |
| bacalao | codfish | lomo | loin |
| besugo | sea bream | manzana | apple |
| bistec | beef steak | mariscos | shellfish |
| boquerones | fresh anchovies | mejillones | mussels |
| caballa | mackerel | melocotón | peach |
| calamares | squid | merluza | hake |
| (a la romana) | (deep fried) | naranja | orange |
| callos | tripe | ostras | oysters |
| cangrejo | crab | pastel | cake |
| caracoles | snails | pescado | fish |
| cebollas | onions | pescadilla | whiting |
| cerdo | pork | pez espada | swordfish |
| champiñones | mushrooms | pimiento | green pepper |
| chorizo | a spicy pork | piña | pineapple |
| | sausage | plátano | banana |
| chuleta | chops | pollo | chicken |
| cordero | lamb | postre | dessert |
| dorada | sea-bass | pulpitos | baby octopus |
| ensalada | salad | queso | cheese |
| entremeses | hors-d'oeuvre | salchichón | salami |
| estofado | stew | salmonete | red mullet |
| filete | fillet | salsa | sauce |
| flan | caramel mould | sandía | watermelon |
| frambuesas | raspberries | sopa | soup |
| fresas | strawberries | ternera | veal |
| frito | fried | tortilla | omelet |
| galletas | biscuits | tostada | toast |
| | (cookies) | trucha | trout |
| gambas | shrimp | uvas | grapes |
| granadas | pomegranates | verduras | vegetables |

# Sports and Other Activities

With hot summers and mild winters, the islands offer an ideal climate for year-round sports activity. Water sports are tops, of course, but landlubbers won't feel left out.

Remember that the Mediterranean sun can be extremely dangerous. If you aren't used to it, three or four hours of mid-afternoon sun will be enough to turn you a bright, painful lobster-red. Take the sun in easy doses—half an hour twice a day is plenty—until you've built up a sun-tan. For the rest of the time wear a tee-shirt or something light to cover your shoulders. A hat and sunglasses are a good idea, too.

Here's a listing of sports to choose from during your holiday on the island:

## BOATING AND SAILING

Most beaches and larger seaside hotels have some kind of water-craft for hire. Prices vary from resort to resort.

*The bliss of warmth and water can be wrecked by overexposure to sun.*

*Gently sloping beaches are a feature of much of Majorca's coastline.*

**Pedalos:** these two-seaters are propelled by foot-driven paddles and are stable enough for young children accompanied by adults.

**Gondolas:** open "banana-boat" type canoe with a seat for one (though two can have a lot of fun). Not suitable for children.

**Sailing dinghies:** a practical little boat for the novice, holding up to three people.

**Windsurfing / Boardsailing:** Masses of possibilities here, all along the coast, and the wind blows hard and strong to keep you skimming along.

## SNORKELLING

The ultra-clear waters of the Balearics make this the ideal spot for snorkellers. The rugged coastlines of Majorca and Minorca conceal bays and inlets many of which are inaccessible except on foot or by boat. On Majorca head for Cala Ratjada, the shores of Cape Formentor or the island of Dragonera. On Minorca, spear-fishermen favour the nooks and crannies between Fornells and Es Grau.

Reasonably priced equipment—from simple masks for

children to high-powered air-operated spear-guns—is available in most resorts on both islands.

## SWIMMING

The islands' most popular sport is obviously swimming. During peak seasons major resorts are packed but between these tourist centres you'll find the beaches much less crowded. Facilities aren't as good on Spanish beaches as in some other countries, though larger beaches have restaurants, showers and changing rooms. Beach chairs may be hired by the day for a very small sum.

Beaches are generally not patrolled by life-guards (although some beaches do have first-aid stations). Keep an even closer watch on children than you normally would.

## WATER SKIING

At water-ski schools, expect to pay a hefty price for 10 minutes of skiing, and the going rate is nearly doubled for a 10-minute lesson. If you are determined to learn this sport during your holiday or if you want a run each day, tell the ski-school chief, and try for a healthy discount.

*Quayside fishing tests fisherman's skill, ingenuity and patience.*

Because island beaches aren't patrolled as strictly as in other countries, swimming and skiing areas gradually overlap as the day goes by. So don't expect a clear run if you are a power-boat driver or a skier—even if you are in the designated ski area.

## FISHING

Fishing from the rocks on the shore is popular, but you'll probably get a bigger haul if you hire a boat and head for the open water. Fishing tackle is cheap and available in most resorts.

## HUNTING AND SHOOTING

A very popular island sport; hunters bag hare, rabbit, duck, quail and partridge. For details about hunting permits, check with local or foreign tourist offices or write to I.C.O.N.A., Carrer Sabino de Arana, 22, Barcelona.

## GOLF

Majorca and Minorca have four golf courses:
**Son Vida Club de Golf,** five kilometres from centre of Palma; 18 holes.
**Club de Golf de Poniente,** 13 kilometres from Palma; 18 holes.
**Club de Golf Santa Ponsa,** at Magaluf, 15 kilometres from Palma; 18 holes.
**Club de Golf Punta Rotja,** at Costa de los Pinos, 65 kilometres from Palma; 9 holes.
**Club de Golf Shangri-la**, four kilometres from Mahón (Minorca); 18 holes.
Caddies and lessons are usually available. Fees are reasonable, and lower on weekdays.

## HORSE RACING

Harness races are held each Sunday from 6 to 10 p.m. and often on public holidays at Palma's Hippodrome fewer than three kilometres north of the city. Also on Minorca there's horse-racing at Estadio Mahones in Mahón, and Estadio Torre del Ram, Ciudadela.

## HORSE-RIDING

There are several ranches on the islands where you can hire horses by the hour or day. Prices are still agreeably inexpensive, with cheaper rates for half-day or full-day hire.

## TENNIS

Many hotels and apartment and villa complexes have their own tennis courts. Fees are charged by the hour and vary according to the category of hotel. In summer you may have to book a day ahead. Some hotels have professionals on the staff who give lessons at generally low rates.

# BLUEPRINT for a Perfect Trip

# How to Get There

Fares and routes for local and international transport—whether by rail, sea, air, road or a combination of these—are constantly changing. Your travel agent should have the most up-to-date information, but the following outline will give you an idea of the various possibilities.

When planning your trip, consult the Blueprint section in this book (pages 95 to 125), especially CUSTOMS AND ENTRY REGULATIONS and HOTELS AND ACCOMMODATION. If perused in advance, this whole section will help you prepare for your visit to Majorca.

## From Great Britain

**BY AIR:** There are daily, non-stop flights from London to Palma; departures are even more frequent in high season. You can also travel to Palma via Paris or Brussels.

Apart from the standard first-class and economy fares, main types of fares available include Moneysaver flights, Budget and Freedom fares.

**Charter Flights and Package Tours:** There is an enormous choice of tours available from all of Britain's major tour operators, and therefore it is wise to consult a reliable travel agent who will be able to assist you in selecting the most suitable standard of hotel, destination and overall package. Prices vary dramatically.

Read your contract carefully before signing. Most travel agents recommend cancellation insurance, a modestly priced safeguard: you lose no money if illness or accident forces you to cancel your holiday.

**Student Flights:** An extensive charter network for students, operating throughout Europe, includes flights to Barcelona, Madrid and Málaga from Britain and other countries. You need an International Student Card to qualify. National or on-campus student travel offices have details.

**BY CAR:** During the summer, when cross-Channel ferry space is at a premium, be sure you have a firm reservation. Special rates and half-fare tickets for children are available at various times on some carriers. Some lines offer discounted round-trip tickets for short excursions. Here's how you can go:

**By car ferry:** The principal routes link Dover and Folkstone with Calais, Boulogne, Dieppe and Dunkirk: Weymouth-Cherbourg; Plymouth-Roscoff; Cork to Roscoff and Le Havre; Newhaven-Dieppe; Portsmouth-St. Malo, Cherbourg and Le Havre; Southampton-Le Havre and Cherbourg; Ramsgate-Dunkirk.

Ferry services between Plymouth and Santander, on the north coast of Spain, have been greatly increased; this route cuts driving time enormously.

**By hovercraft:** In around 35–40 minutes you can cross from Dover to Calais.

Car ferries operate daily all year round between Majorca and Barcelona (an eight-hour trip); extra boats are put on in high season. Ferries connect Alicante and Valencia with Majorca. Reservations for vehicle space may be difficult in the high season, so book far in advance.

**By air:** It's more expensive, but you and your car can fly from Southend to Le Touquet. Once in France, British motorists usually need some time to become accustomed to driving on the right. It's also wise to proceed very carefully while taking the measure of the French drivers, who are reckless by British or American standards.

The route through Paris is almost entirely toll motorway to the Spanish frontier. The Spanish motorway, called *Autopista del Mediterráneo*, now runs as far as Alicante.

**BY RAIL:** Good, though crowded, trains link Spain and Great Britain. Seat and sleeper reservations are compulsory. Passengers will have to change trains at the Spanish frontier as the Spanish tracks have a wider gauge than those on most of the Continent. The only exceptions are the EuroCity and the Talgo, which have adjustable axles. The best way is to travel as far as Barcelona by train, then continue to Majorca by air or by sea. The Spanish Tourist Office can give you details on discounted fares within the Spanish rail network. Other reduced price tickets:

**Eurailpass:** North Americans—in fact, anyone except residents of Europe—can travel on a flat-rate, unlimited mileage ticket valid for first-class rail travel anywhere in western Europe outside of Great Britain. The Eurailpass may be purchased for periods of 2 or 3 weeks, 1, 2 or 3 months. Eurail Youthpass offers 1 or 2 months of second-class travel to anyone under 26. These tickets also offer discounts on other forms of transportation. You must buy your pass before leaving home.

**Inter-Rail Card:** This ticket permits 30 days of unlimited rail travel in participating European countries and Morocco to people under 26. In the country of issue, fares are given a 50% discount.

**BY COACH:** Europabus services to Barcelona are offered from London via Ostend and Brussels. Relatively cheap, but the trip can be tiring. From Barcelona, domestic air or sea transport to Majorca is easy. Travel agents have the details.

## From North America

**BY AIR:** There are non-stop flights from New York to Barcelona with connecting flights to Palma. You can also travel from New York, Boston, Washington, etc., via Madrid or another European gateway city, with the possibility of making a stopover.

On scheduled airlines the fare is reduced if you sign up for a transatlantic excursion of a specified period. Extra stops may be taken but there will probably be an additional charge.

The APEX (Advance Purchase Excursion) fare must be booked and ticketed well in advance and is subject to a cancellation penalty. Children can fly for two-thirds of the adult rate.

**Charter Flights and Package Tours:** ABC (Advance Booking Charter) flights cost slightly less than APEX fares but go to fewer destinations: tickets must be bought a month or 6 weeks in advance, depending on the destination. Travel agents offer OTC (One-Stop Tour Inclusive Charter) packages, that combine air travel with hotel and other ground arrangements at bargain prices. These flights are open to all.

# When to Go

Like the other Balearic islands, Majorca enjoys a moderate climate all year round. A wall of rugged mountains, running along its northern coast, protects it from cold winds. Even in the depths of winter, the weather is quite bearable—though, of course, considerably cooler than in summer. It rarely freezes, but it can turn chilly in high season as well as in the winter months. Be prepared with some warm clothing.

Majorca boasts about 300 sunny days a year—with an average of five hours of sunshine per day in the winter, ten in summer.

The average daily temperatures, indicated below, will help you decide when you want to plan your visit to Majorca and what you should take along in the way of clothing.

|  |  | J | F | M | A | M | J | J | A | S | O | N | D |
|---|---|---|---|---|---|---|---|---|---|---|---|---|---|
| **Maximum** | °F | 57 | 59 | 62 | 66 | 71 | 79 | 84 | 84 | 80 | 73 | 65 | 59 |
|  | °C | 14 | 15 | 17 | 19 | 22 | 26 | 29 | 29 | 27 | 23 | 18 | 15 |
| **Minimum** | °F | 43 | 44 | 46 | 51 | 55 | 62 | 67 | 68 | 65 | 57 | 50 | 46 |
|  | °C | 6 | 6 | 8 | 10 | 13 | 17 | 20 | 20 | 18 | 14 | 10 | 8 |
| **Days of sunshine** |  | 15 | 14 | 16 | 19 | 20 | 22 | 28 | 26 | 20 | 16 | 14 | 14 |

All figures shown are approximate monthly averages.

# Planning Your Budget

To give you an idea of what to expect, here are some average prices in Spanish pesetas. However, they must be regarded as approximate, as inflation creeps relentlessly up. Prices quoted may be subject to a VAT/sales tax (I.V.A.) of either 6 or 12%.

**Airport transfer.** Majorca: bus from Son San Juan airport to Palma 100 ptas., taxi about 900–1,000 ptas. Minorca: taxi from airport to Mahón centre about 900 ptas.

**Baby-sitters.** 800–1,000 ptas. per hour.

**Bicycle and motorscooter hire.** Bicycle per day 500 ptas., moped per day 2,500 ptas., scooter per day about 3,000 ptas.

**Car hire** (unlimited mileage). *Seat Ibiza 1.2* 5,000 ptas. per day, 30,000 ptas. per week. *Ford Escort* 6,000 ptas. per day, 36,000 ptas. per week. Add. 12% tax.

**Cigarettes.** Spanish brands 47–110 ptas. per packet of 20, foreign brands 175–250 ptas.

**Entertainment.** Bullfight 2,000 ptas. and up, cinema 300 ptas. and up, flamenco nightclub show 1,200–2,000 ptas. and up, discotheque (admission and first drink) 500 ptas. and up.

**Hairdressers.** *Woman's* haircut 1,500–2,500 ptas., shampoo and set or blow-dry 900–1,200 ptas. *Man's* haircut 800–1,200 ptas.

**Hotels** (double room with bath). ***** 10,000–15,000 ptas. **** 3,000–10,500 ptas., *** 6,500 ptas., ** 4,500 ptas., * 3,000 ptas.

**Meals and drinks.** Continental breakfast 400–500 ptas., *plato del día* from 500–600 ptas., lunch/dinner in good establishment 1,600 ptas. and up, beer (small bottle or glass) 100–150 ptas., coffee 80–125 ptas., Spanish brandy 150 ptas., soft drinks 100 ptas. and up.

**Shopping bag.** Loaf of bread 60–150 ptas., 200 grams of butter 250 ptas., 6 eggs 120 ptas., beefsteak (500 g.) 750 ptas., 250 grams of coffee 300 ptas., 100 grams of instant coffee 415–425 ptas., fruit juice (1 litre) 200–230 ptas., bottle of wine 150 ptas. and up.

**Sports.** *Golf* (per day) green fee 1,600–3,000 ptas. *Tennis* court fee 500 ptas. per hour. *Horse-riding* from 3,000 ptas. per half-day. *Water skiing* about 1,000 ptas. per round, from 3,500 ptas. per hour for lesson.

# An A–Z Summary of Practical Information and Facts

> A star (*) following an entry indicates that relevant prices are to be found on page 100.
>
> Listed after most main entries is the appropriate Spanish translation, usually in the singular, plus a number of phrases that may come in handy during your stay in Majorca.

## AIRPORTS* *(aeropuerto)* **A**

**Majorca.** Son San Juan airport has two terminals; one handles scheduled flights, the other is reserved for charter flights. Porters are always available to carry bags to the taxi rank and bus stop. They charge an official rate, which is paid per piece of luggage.

A tourist information office, hotel-reservation, car-hire and currency-exchange counters, a post office, restaurant, bar, hairdresser, luggage deposit, duty-free shop and souvenir shops are at your disposal. Taxis and coaches link Son San Juan Airport with Palma, a 15-minute trip. Official taxi fares are posted by the airport exit doors. The coach service operates to Palma Railway Station—Estación de Ferrocarriles—at Plaza de España every half hour from early morning till around midnight. Hotel coaches meet charter-flight passengers.

**Minorca.** Taxis and buses serve Mahón Airport, only 5 kilometres from Mahón. Air terminal facilities are limited.

| | |
|---|---|
| Where's the bus for ..? | **¿De dónde sale el autobús para ..?** |

## BABY-SITTERS. **B**

The larger hotels provide this facility as a matter of course. Prices depend on the time of day and the length of the engagement. Tourists on a package holiday can make arrangements for baby-sitting at their travel agency.

| | |
|---|---|
| Can you get me a baby-sitter for tonight? | **¿Puede conseguirme una canguro para cuidar los niños esta noche?** |

## BICYCLE and MOTORSCOOTER HIRE* *(bicicletas/scooters de alquiler).*

The most practical and enjoyable way to explore the islands

**B**  is to hire a bicycle – or a tandem model. Mopeds (motorbikes) and motorscooters are also available at widely varying rates, but you'll need a licence exclusively for mopeds and motorscooters. Remember that the use of crash helmets is compulsory when driving a motorcycle, whatever the capacity of the engine.

| | |
|---|---|
| I'd like to hire a bicycle. | **Quisiera alquilar una bicicleta.** |
| What's the charge per day/week? | **¿Cuánto cobran por día/semana?** |

**C**  **CAMPING** *(camping)*. There is a good campsite at Ca'n Picafort on Majorca (but it's the only one on the island), 2 kilometres from the centre of the town on a main road served by plenty of buses. You may also be able to camp on private land, but be sure to ask permission of the owner first.

| | |
|---|---|
| May we camp here? | **¿Podemos acampar aquí?** |
| We've a tent. | **Tenemos una tienda de camping.** |

**CAR HIRE\*** *(coches de alquiler)*. There are car hire firms in most tourist resorts and main towns. The law requires that you have an International Driving Licence. However, if you are stopped by the police, your national driving licence may be enough. It's up to you whether you want to take a chance. You must also be over 18 or 21, if not 25, and have had your licence at least six months.

The most common type of car available for hire is the Seat (pronounced SAY-at). Rates vary, so it's a good idea to shop around. Those given on page 100 are sample prices of major operators.

In the Balearics, unlimited free mileage is always included in the contract.

General conditions may include a refundable deposit, but holders of major credit cards are normally exempt.

A sales tax is added to the total rental charge.

| | |
|---|---|
| I'd like to rent a car (tomorrow). | **Quisiera alquilar un coche (para mañana).** |
| for one day/a week | **por un día/una semana** |
| Please include full insurance. | **Haga el favor de incluir el seguro a todo riesgo.** |

**CHILDREN'S ACTIVITIES.** Visitors travelling with young children are welcome all over Spain, and Majorca and Minorca are no exception. Following are some suggestions for outings on Majorca with the children, which parents will enjoy, too:

**Puerto Sóller** (25 km. from Palma) delights old and young alike with its narrow-gauge tram line, linking the port to the picturesque town of Sóller several miles inland. You make the journey in quaint carriages that date from the turn of the century.

**Porto Cristo** (60 km. from Palma) is a quiet family resort situated on a long beach. The sea here is calm and shallow, providing safe swimming for children. Other attractions in the vicinity include an aquarium and a series of caves which can be explored by boat and a drive round the Safari Park (see p. 83).

**La Granja** (near Esporlas) gives an idea of farm life on Majorca in the days before mechanization. Costumed workers demonstrate traditional island handicrafts — including lace making, ceramics, weaving and spinning — as well as the forging of iron and the churning of butter. Folk dances are performed on the grounds and donkey rides are another popular attraction.

The beach is the ideal place to keep a child amused. Pedalos, gondolas and small boats can be hired at many beaches, though few have lifeguards, so you will have to keep an eye on your children yourself.

If you should lose your child on the beach or elsewhere, go either to the municipal police station or the Guardia Civil headquarters. Happily, Spaniards are particularly fond of children and will go out of their way to help them. It would be unusual for a Spaniard to pass by a child who was crying and obviously lost.

**CIGARETTES, CIGARS, TOBACCO\*** *(cigarrillos, puros, tabaco).* Spanish cigarettes can be made of strong, black tobacco *(negro)* or light tobacco *(rubio).*

*Ducados* are popular for filtered black tobacco; *Fortuna, Nobel* (filter) and *Bisonte* (non-filter) resemble foreign light blends. Nearly all popular foreign brands are sold at twice to three times the price of the domestic product.

Spanish cigars are not expensive; Cuban cigars are readily available.

Most foreigners feel Spanish pipe tobacco is a bit on the rough side. Imported tobacco, sometimes hard to find, is expensive.

| | |
|---|---|
| A packet of …/A box of matches, please. | **Un paquete de …/Una caja de cerillas, por favor.** |
| filter-tipped | **con filtro** |
| without filter | **sin filtro** |

103

**C** **CLOTHING and PACKING.** From June to September you can count on hot weather every day, but pack a jacket or cardigan for the occasional cool evening. The most comfortable clothing for hot weather is of cotton or other natural fibres, as these are cooler and absorb perspiration better. During the rest of the year evenings can be cold, and you will need heavier clothes.

In Spain, where wearing a bikini was once considered daring, topless bathing has become fairly common. Though officially a misdemeanour, the authorities usually turn the other way—if it's done discreetly.

Sober clothing—no Bermuda shorts or very short skirts—should, of course, be worn when visiting churches. Note that women no longer *have* to cover their heads.

There is no need to pack a vast supply of toothpaste, soap, sun-tan oils or lotions, mosquito repellents, etc. All the usual brands are sold on the islands, though prices in resorts may be higher than in the towns.

| | |
|---|---|
| Will I need a jacket and tie? | **¿Necesito chaqueta y corbata?** |
| Is it all right if I wear this? | **¿Voy bien así?** |

**COMMUNICATIONS.** Post offices *(correos)* are for mail and telegrams only; normally you can't make telephone calls from them.

**Post office hours:** 9 a.m. to 2 p.m., Monday to Friday; 9 a.m. to 1 p.m., Saturdays. The main post office is also open from 4 to 7 p.m. (9 a.m. to 7 p.m. for stamps).

Small parcels can be mailed from local post offices. Heavier ones must be sent from the main post offices in Palma or Mahón.

**Mail:** If you don't know in advance where you'll be staying, you can have your mail addressed to the *Lista de Correos* (poste restante or general delivery) in the nearest town:

> Mr. John Smith
> Lista de Correos
> Sóller
> Majorca, Baleares
> Spain

Take your passport with you to the post office for identification. Postage stamps *(sello)* are also on sale at tobacconists *(tabacos)* and often at hotel desks.

Mailboxes are yellow.

**Telegrams** *(telegrama):* The main telegraph office in Palma is at: **C**
Constitucio; tel. 72 20 00

In Mahón you'll find it at Buen Aire, 15; tel. 36 38 95

**Telephone** *(teléfono)*: The telephone office is almost always independent of the local post office. It is identified by a blue and white sign. Major towns and many tourist centres have automatic dialling facilities for local, inter-urban and some international calls. Area or STD code numbers are given in the telephone directory. In smaller towns and villages where phones are not yet automatic you'll have to go through the operator. To reverse the charges ask for *cobro revertido*. For a personal (person-to-person) call, specify *persona a persona*.

To make a call from a telephone booth, you'll need a supply of 5-, 25-, 50- and 100-peseta coins.

For international direct dialling, pick up the receiver, wait for the dial tone, then dial 07, wait for a second sound and dial the country code, city code and subscriber's number.

| Telephone Spelling Code | | | |
|---|---|---|---|
| **A** Antonio | **G** Gerona | **M** Madrid | **S** Sábado |
| **B** Barcelona | **H** Historia | **N** Navarra | **T** Tarragona |
| **C** Carmen | **I** Inés | **Ñ** Ñoño | **U** Ulises |
| **CH** Chocolate | **J** José | **O** Oviedo | **V** Valencia |
| **D** Dolores | **K** Kilo | **P** Paris | **W** Washington |
| **E** Enrique | **L** Lorenzo | **Q** Querido | **X** Xiquena |
| **F** Francia | **LL** Llobregat | **R** Ramón | **Y** Yegua |
| | | | **Z** Zaragoza |

| | |
|---|---|
| Have you received any mail for me? | **¿Ha recibido correo para mí?** |
| A stamp for this letter/postcard, please. | **Por favor, un sello para esta carta/tarjeta.** |
| express (special delivery) | **urgente** |
| airmail | **vía aérea** |
| registered | **certificado** |
| I want to send a telegram to … | **Quisiera mandar un telegrama a …** |
| Can you get me this number in …? | **¿Puede comunicarme con este número en … ?** |

**C** **COMPLAINTS.** By law, all hotels, campsites and restaurants must have official complaint forms *(Hoja Oficial de Reclamación/Full Oficial de Reclamació)* and produce them on demand. The original of this triplicate document should be sent to the regional office of the Ministry of Tourism, one copy remains with the establishment complained against and you keep the third sheet. Merely asking for a complaint form is usually enough to resolve most matters since tourism authorities take a serious view of complaints and your host wants to keep both his reputation and his licence.

New legislation has been introduced that greatly strengthens the consumer's hand. Public information offices are being set up, controls carried out, and fallacious information made punishable by law. For a tourist's needs, however, the tourist office, or in really serious cases, the police would normally be able to handle or, at least, to advise where to go.

### CONSULATES *(consulado)*

**Great Britain:*** Plaza Mayor, 3-D, Palma; tel. 71 24 45

**Canada:** For minor matters see British consulate, Palma. All other cases: Consulate General, Edif. Goya, Calle Núñez de Balboa, 35, Madrid, tel. 225 91 19

**Eire:** Gran Via Carles III, 94, Barcelona; tel. 431 43 00

**U.S.A.** (vice-consulate): Avda. Rei Jaume III, 26, Palma; tel. 72 26 60

| | |
|---|---|
| Where's the British/American consulate? | **¿Dónde está el consulado británico/americano ?** |

### CONVERTER CHARTS.
For fluid and distance measures, see pp. 109 and 110. Spain uses the metric system.

**Temperature**

°C  −30 −25 −20 −15 −10 −5  0   5   10  15  20  25  30  35  40  45
°F      −20 −10  0   10  20  30  40  50  60  70  80  90  100 110

* Also for citizens of Commonwealth countries.

# Length

| cm | 0 | 5 | 10 | 15 | 20 | 25 | 30 |
|---|---|---|---|---|---|---|---|
| inches | 0 | 2 | 4 | 6 | 8 | 10 | 12 |

| meters | 0 | | 1 m | | 2 m |
|---|---|---|---|---|---|
| ft./yd. | 0 | 1 ft. | 1 yd. | 2 yd. | |

# Weight

| grams | 0 | 100 | 200 | 300 | 400 | 500 | 600 | 700 | 800 | 900 | 1 kg |
|---|---|---|---|---|---|---|---|---|---|---|---|
| ounces | 0 | 4 | 8 | 12 | 1 lb | 20 | 24 | 28 | 2 lb. | | |

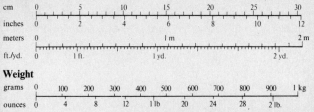

**CRIME and THEFT.** Spain's crime rate is catching up with the rest of the world. Thefts and break-ins are increasing. Hang on to purses and wallets, especially in busy places—the bullfight, open air markets, fiestas. Don't take valuables to the beach. Lock cars and *never* leave cases, cameras, etc., on view. If you suffer a theft or break-in, report it to the Guardia Civil. Tourists should be on their guard in the area around Palma's Plaza Mayor by day. After dark, this section of town is best avoided altogether, even if you're in a small group.

I want to report a theft.
**Quiero denunciar un robo.**
My ticket/wallet/passport has been stolen.
**Me han robado el billete/ la cartera/el pasaporte.**

**CUSTOMS and ENTRY REGULATIONS.** Most visitors, including citizens of Great Britain, the U.S.A., Canada and Eire, require only a valid passport to enter Spain. Visitors from Australia, New Zealand and South Africa, however, must have visas. If in doubt, check with your travel agent before departure. Tourists are generally entitled to stay in Spain up to 90 days; Americans can remain for 180 days. If you expect to stay longer, a Spanish consulate or tourist office can advise you.

In addition to personal clothing and jewellery, the following items are also allowed: enough perfume for personal use, two still cameras, one cine film camera, one video camera, one video recorder, one portable TV, one portable radio, one portable record player, one portable typewriter, one portable tape or cassette recorder, one pair of binoculars. (For some items, you may have to fill in a form guaranteeing you won't sell the item while in Spain. Or you may have to put up a deposit which will be returned when you leave the country).

The following chart shows the main duty-free items that you can bring into Spain and, when returning home, into your own country:

**C**

| Into: | Cigarettes | | Cigars | | Tobacco | | Spirits | Wine |
|---|---|---|---|---|---|---|---|---|
| Spain 1) | 300 | or | 75 | or | 350 g. | | 1.5 l. and | 5 l. |
| 2) | 200 | or | 50 | or | 250 g. | | 1 l. or | 2 l. |
| Australia | 200 | or | 50 | or | 250 g. | | 1 l. or | 1 l. |
| Canada | 200 | and | 50 | and | 900 g. | | 1.1 l. or | 1.1 l. |
| Eire | 200 | or | 50 | or | 250 g. | | 1 l. and | 2 l. |
| N. Zealand | 200 | or | 50 | or | 250 g. | | 1.1 l. and | 4.5 l. |
| S. Africa | 400 | and | 50 | and | 250 g. | | 1 l. and | 2 l. |
| U.K. | 200 | or | 50 | or | 250 g. | | 1 l. and | 2 l. |
| U.S.A. | 200 | and | 100 | and | 3) | | 1 l. or | 1 l. |

1) Visitors arriving from EEC countries.
2) Visitors arriving from other countries.
3) A reasonable quantity.

**Currency restrictions.** Tourists may bring an unlimited amount of Spanish or foreign currency into the country. Departing, though, you must declare any amount beyond the equivalent of 500,000 pesetas. Thus if you plan to carry large sums in and out again it's wise to declare your currency on arrival as well as on departure.

**D** **DRIVING IN SPAIN.** To take your car into Spain, you should have:

- an International Driving Permit (not obligatory for citizens of most Western European countries—ask your automobile association— but recommended in case of difficulties with the police as it carries a text in Spanish) or a legalized and certified translation of your driving licence
- car registration papers
- Green Card (an extension to your regular insurance policy, making it valid for foreign countries.

*Also recommended:* With your certificate of insurance, you should carry a bail bond. If you injure somebody in an accident in Spain, you can be imprisoned while the accident is under investigation. This bond will bail you out. Apply to your automobile association or insurance company.

**Driving conditions on Majorca and Minorca:** The rules are the same as in mainland Spain and the rest of the Continent: drive on the right, overtake (pass) on the left, yield right of way to all vehicles coming from the right. If your car has seat belts, it's obligatory to use them; fines for non-compliance are high.

There is an expanding motorway network, and all major roads on the islands are well surfaced. Secondary roads in Majorca are narrow but good; in Minorca they can be rough, potholed and very badly signposted. On both islands roads marked as cart roads or tracks may be negotiable only with difficulty.

Be warned that quaint local attractions can become deadly perils on the road—horse-drawn carts, donkeys, sheep, goats and old folk who haven't quite adapted to the age of the automobile. When passing through villages, drive with extra care to avoid children darting out of doorways and older folk strolling in the middle of the road, particularly after dark.

**Traffic police:** The roads are patrolled by motorcycle police of the Civil Guard *(Guardia Civil)*. They always ride in pairs and are armed. They are noted for their courtesy but can be tough on lawbreakers. Fines are payable on the spot. You might be stopped for:

- speeding
- travelling too close to the car in front
- overtaking (passing) without flashing your direction indicator lights
- travelling at night with a burnt-out light (Spanish law requires you to carry a complete set of spare bulbs at all times).
- failing to come to a complete halt at a STOP sign.

**Fuel and oil:** Service stations are now plentiful in most tourist areas of Majorca, but not Minorca. There you'd best check your tank before crossing the island.

Petrol (gasoline) available is 92, 95 (lead-free) and 97 octane and diesel fuel.

**Fluid measures**

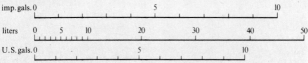

**Breakdowns:** Balearic garages are as efficient as any, but in tourist areas major repairs may take several days because of the heavy work- 109

**D** load. Spare parts are readily available for Spanish-built cars. For other makes, spares may have to be imported, so have your car checked before the journey.

**Distance**

| km | 0 | 1 | 2 | 3 | 4 | 5 | 6 | 8 | 10 | 12 | 14 | 16 |
|---|---|---|---|---|---|---|---|---|---|---|---|---|
| miles | 0 | ½ | 1 | 1½ | 2 | 3 | 4 | 5 | 6 | 7 | 8 | 9 | 10 |

**Road signs:** Most road signs are the standard pictographs used throughout Europe. However, you may encounter these written signs:

| | |
|---|---|
| **¡Alto!** | Halt! |
| **Aparcamiento** | Parking |
| **Autopista (de peaje)** | (Toll) motorway/expressway |
| **Calzada deteriorada** | Bad road |
| **Calzada estrecha** | Narrow road |
| **Ceda el paso** | Give way (Yield) |
| **Cruce peligroso** | Dangerous crossroads |
| **Cuidado** | Caution |
| **Curva peligrosa** | Dangerous bend |
| **Despacio** | Slow |
| **Desviación** | Diversion (Detour) |
| **Escuela** | School |
| **Obras** | Road works (Men working) |
| **¡Pare!** | Stop! |
| **Peligro** | Danger |
| **Prohibido adelantar** | No overtaking (passing) |
| **Prohibido aparcar** | No parking |
| **Puesto de socorro** | First-aid post |

| | |
|---|---|
| (International) Driving Licence | **carné de conducir (internacional)** |
| Car registration papers | **permiso de circulación** |
| Green Card | **carta verde** |

| | |
|---|---|
| Are we on the right road for …? | **¿Es ésta la carretera hacia …?** |
| Fill the tank please, top grade. | **Llénelo, por favor, con super.** |
| Check the oil/tires/battery. | **Por favor, controle el aceite/ los neumáticos/la batería.** |

| | |
|---|---|
| I've had a breakdown. | **Mi coche se ha estropeado.** |
| There's been an accident. | **Ha habido un accidente** |

**DRUGS.** Until the 1980s, Spain had one of the strictest drug laws in Europe. Then possession of small quantities for personal use was legalized. Now the pendulum has swung back in the other direction: possession and sale of drugs is once again a criminal offense in Spain.

**ELECTRIC CURRENT** *(corriente eléctrica)*. 220 volt A.C. is becoming standard, but older installations of 125 volts can still be found. Check before plugging in. If the voltage is 125, American appliances (i.e. razors) built for 60 cycles will run on 50-cycle European current, but more slowly.

| | |
|---|---|
| What's the voltage—125 or 220? | **¿Cuál es el voltaje—ciento veinticinco (125) o doscientos veinte (220)?** |
| an adaptor | **un adaptador** |
| a battery | **una pila** |

**EMERGENCIES.** If you're not staying at a hotel, ring or visit the local Municipal Police or the Guardia Civil. If possible take a Spanish speaker with you. Depending on the nature of the emergency, refer to the separate entries in this book, such as CONSULATES, MEDICAL CARE, POLICE, etc.

Here are a few important telephone numbers:

| | Majorca | Minorca |
|---|---|---|
| Police | 091 | 091 |
| First aid *(Casa de socorro)* | 722179 (Palma) | 361221 (Mahón) |
| Fire *(bomberos)* | 080 (Palma) | 363961 (Mahón) |

Though we hope you'll never need them, here are a few key words you might like to learn in advance:

| | | | |
|---|---|---|---|
| Careful | **Cuidado** | Police | **Policía** |
| Fire | **Fuego** | Stop | **Deténgase** |
| Help | **Socorro** | Stop thief | **Al ladrón** |

**FIRE** *(incendio)*. Forest fires are a menace in Majorca, particularly in the mountainous north-east where the only way to fight them may be aerial bombardment with chemicals. So be very careful where you throw your matches and cigarette butts. Campers must douse fires with water and cover them with earth before moving on.

**GUIDES and INTERPRETERS.** Apply to the Grupo Sindical de Informadores Turísticos:
Miguel Marqués, 13, Palma; tel. 460930.

**G**  In Minorca a list of individual guides and interpreters is available at the
Delegación Insular del Ministerio de Información y Turismo, Plaza de la Esplanada, 48, Mahón; tel 36 08 79.

| | |
|---|---|
| We'd like an English-speaking guide. | **Queremos un guía que hable inglés.** |
| I need an English interpreter. | **Necesito un intérprete de inglés.** |

**H**  **HAGGLING.** It's pointless to bargain in shops because merchants who post their prices stick to them. But you may discreetly ask for a discount on very large purchases. Haggling is customary, however, at flea markets or similar places.

**HAIRDRESSERS\*** *(peluquería)*/**BARBERS** *(barbería)*. Many hotels have their own salons, and the standard is generally good. Prices vary widely according to the class of the establishment. Most include a service charge in the price, but it is customary to give an additional tip of 10%.

The following vocabulary will help:

| | |
|---|---|
| I'd like a shampoo and set. | **Quiero lavado y marcado.** |
| I want a ... | **Quiero ...** |
| haircut | **un corte de pelo** |
| razor cut | **un corte a navaja** |
| blow-dry (brushing) | **un modelado** |
| permanent wave | **una permanente** |
| colour rinse/hair-dye | **reflejos/un tinte** |
| manicure | **una manicura** |
| Don't cut it too short. | **No me lo corte mucho.** |
| A little more off (here). | **Un poco más (aquí).** |

**HITCH-HIKING** *(auto-stop)*. In Spain, hitch-hiking is permitted everywhere.

| | |
|---|---|
| Can you give me/us a lift to ...? | **¿Puede llevarme/llevarnos a ...?** |

**HOTELS and ACCOMMODATION\***. Hotel prices have been freed
112 from government control. Accommodation in the Balearics ranges

from a simple room in a *pensión* (boarding house) to the more luxurious surroundings of a resort hotel.

Before a guest takes up a room, he fills out a form stating the hotel category, room number, price and signs it. Breakfast is normally included in the room rate.

However, the overwhelming majority of tourists who arrive in the islands have reserved and paid for their accommodation in advance through package-tour operators abroad. Tourists arriving without reservations at the height of the summer season may be hard pressed to find adequate lodging. Off-season rates are theoretically lower, and vacancies, of course, are much more numerous (see also WHEN TO GO, page 98).

## Other forms of accommodation

**Hostal:** Modest hotels, often family concerns, graded by stars (one to three).

**Pensión:** Boarding houses, graded one to three, with few amenities.

**Fonda:** Village inns, clean and unpretentious.

All hotels have complaint forms *(hoja de reclamaciones)* in case you are dissatisfied (see COMPLAINTS).

Increasingly popular in Mediterranean tourism is a package arrangement, including a furnished apartment or villa. The cost is little more than the scheduled air fare alone. Arrangements often have to be made well in advance.

**Youth Hostels** *(albergue de juventud)*: There is a youth hostel at Playa de Palma, tel. 260892. Otherwise, students will easily find lodging at pennywise rates.

| | |
|---|---|
| a double/single room | **una habitación doble/sencilla** |
| with bath/shower | **con baño/ducha** |
| What's the rate per night? | **¿Cuál es el precio por noche?** |

**HOURS.** Schedules here revolve around the siesta, one of the really great Spanish discoveries, aimed at keeping people out of the midday sun. The word has become universal; unfortunately, the custom hasn't. But when in Spain you should certainly try it.

To accommodate the midday pause most shops and offices are open from 9 a.m. to 1.30 p.m. and then from 4.30 p.m. (5 in winter) to 8, 9 or 10 p.m.

Restaurants serve lunch between 1 and 3.30 p.m. and dinner—earlier than on the mainland—between 8 and 10 p.m.

**L** **LANGUAGE.** Majorca and Minorca are bilingual islands. The national language of Spain, Castilian Spanish, is understood everywhere. But in addition, *Mallorquí* is spoken in Majorca and *Menorquí* in Minorca. These are island dialects of Catalan, a Romance language common to eastern Spain and the French Pyrenees.

Many islanders speak Castilian with a marked, yet clear accent. Some foreigners, struggling along with school Spanish, find it easier to understand than purer mainland accents.

Some English is spoken in resort towns, but rarely in country districts. French or German can prove useful as back-up languages.

|  | **Majorcan** | **Castilian** |
|---|---|---|
| Good morning | *Bon día* | *Buenos días* |
| Good evening | *Bona tarda* | *Buenas tardes* |
| Please | *Si us plau* | *Por favor* |
| Thank you | *Gràcies* | *Gracias* |
| Goodbye | *Adéu* | *Adiós* |

And everywhere you'll hear an indispensable, all-purpose Spanish expression. Said with a shrug, it can mean anything from "you're welcome" to "who cares?" The phrase is: *es igual.*

The Berlitz phrase book, SPANISH FOR TRAVELLERS, covers most situations you're likely to encounter in your travels through the islands. And the Berlitz Spanish–English/English–Spanish pocket dictionary contains a 12,500-word glossary of each language, plus a menu-reader supplement.

| | |
|---|---|
| Do you speak English? | **¿Habla usted inglés?** |
| I don't speak Spanish. | **No hablo español.** |

**LAUNDRY** *(lavandería)* **and DRY-CLEANING** *(tintorería).* Most hotels will handle laundry and dry-cleaning, but they'll usually charge more than an independent establishment.

You'll find self-service launderettes in a few areas.

| | |
|---|---|
| Where's the nearest laundry/dry-cleaners? | **¿Dónde está la lavandería/ tintorería más cercana?** |
| When will it be ready? | **¿Cuándo estará listo?** |
| I must have this for tomorrow morning. | **Lo necesito para mañana por la mañana.** |

**LOST PROPERTY.** The first thing to do when you discover you've lost something is, obviously, to retrace your steps. If nothing comes to light, report the loss to the Municipal Police or the Guardia Civil.

| | |
|---|---|
| I've lost my wallet/handbag/passport. | **He perdido mi cartera/bolso/pasaporte.** |

**MAPS and PLACE NAMES.** With the resurgence of the Catalan language, many places previously known by a Spanish name now have a local equivalent. Both Spanish and local names may be used interchangeably, causing tourists a lot of confusion.

Maps cannot unfortunately keep up with this evolution, so, with the above in mind, it's worth enquiring immediately of a local inhabitant if you can't find a certain place, sight or street you're looking for.

The maps in this guide were prepared by Falk-Verlag, which also publish a map of Majorca.

| | |
|---|---|
| a street plan of ... | **un plano de la ciudad de ...** |
| a road map of the island | **un mapa de carreteras de la isla** |

**MEDICAL CARE.** With the island's climate and adequate standards of hygiene, most tourists who suffer illness have only themselves to blame. Too much sun, food or drink—more likely a combination of all three—have ruined many a holiday. Moderation is the most sensible course.

To be completely at ease, make certain your health insurance policy covers any illness or accident while on holiday. Your travel agent can also fix you up with Spanish tourist insurance (ASTES), but it is a slow-moving process. ASTES covers doctors' fees and clinical care in the event of accident or illness. The cost is calculated according to the length of holiday.

There are doctors in all towns and their consulting hours are displayed. For less serious matters, first-aid personnel, called *practicantes*, make daily rounds of the major tourist hotels, just in case. Away from your hotel, don't hesitate to ask the police or a tourist information office for help. At your hotel, ask the staff to help you.

## M Hospitals

**Majorca:** Clínica Femenia, Calle Camilo José Cela, 20, Palma de Mallorca.

**Minorca:** Hospital Municipal, Cos de Gracia, Mahón.

*Farmacias* (chemists' shops) are usually open during normal shopping hours. After hours, at least one per town remains open all night, and its location is given in the window of all other *farmacias.*

| | |
|---|---|
| a dentist | **un dentista** |
| a doctor | **un médico** |
| an ambulance | **una ambulancia** |
| hospital | **hospital** |
| an upset stomach | **molestias de estómago** |
| sunstroke | **una insolación** |
| a fever | **fiebre** |

**MEETING PEOPLE.** The Spanish, as a whole, are one of the world's most open and hospitable people, easy to talk to and approach, generous to a fault.

The Majorcans are Catalans, and as such form part of the more industrious and wealthier north of the country. Attitudes are less extreme, more down to earth. But there could never be a second's doubt in your mind that you're in Spain, even if it's simply by the noise-level of conversations, quite deafening over any length of time. But what you perhaps take for a quarrel is more often than not simply news and gossip being transmitted... passionately.

Spain's strict moral attitudes still apply in the Balearics, although tourism has loosened the rules. If a pretty local girl should smile at an admirer, it should not be taken as an invitation. Spanish men, on the contrary, consider all foreign women to be fair game.

| | |
|---|---|
| How are you? | **¿Cómo está usted?** |

## MONEY MATTERS

**Currency:** The monetary unit of Spain is the *peseta* (abbreviated *pta.*).

Coins: 1, 2, 5, 10, 25, 50 and 100 pesetas.

Banknotes: 100, 200, 500, 1,000, 2,000 and 5,000 pesetas.

A 5-peseta coin is traditionally called a *duro*, so if someone should quote a price as 10 duros, he means 50 pesetas. For currency restrictions, see CUSTOMS AND ENTRY REGULATIONS.

**Banking hours:** Banks generally open from 9 a.m. to 2 p.m. Monday to Saturday, though some close at 1.30 p.m. in summer.

**Exchange offices:** Outside normal banking hours, many travel agencies and other businesses displaying a *cambio* sign will change foreign currency into pesetas. The exchange rate is a bit less favourable than in the banks. Both banks and exchange offices pay slightly more for traveller's cheques than for cash. Always take your passport with you when you go to change money.

**Credit cards:** All the internationally recognized cards are accepted by hotels, restaurants and businesses in Spain.

**Eurocheques:** You'll have no problem settling bills or paying for purchases with Eurocheques.

**Traveller's cheques:** In tourist areas, shops and all banks, hotels and travel agencies accept them, though you're likely to get a better exchange rate at a national or regional bank. It is certainly safer to hold your holiday funds in cheques. Only cash small amounts at a time, and keep the balance of your cheques in the hotel safe if possible. At the very least, be sure to keep your receipt and a list of the serial numbers of the cheques in a separate place to facilitate a refund in case of loss or theft. Always remember to take your passport with you if you expect to cash a traveller's cheque.

**Paying cash:** Although many shops and bars will accept payment in sterling or dollars, you're better off paying in pesetas. Shops will invariably give you less than the bank rate for foreign currency.

| | |
|---|---|
| Where's the nearest bank/ currency exchange office? | **¿Dónde está el banco/la oficina de cambio más cercana?** |
| I want to change some pounds/dollars. | **Quiero cambiar libras/dólares.** |
| Do you accept traveller's cheques? | **¿Acepta usted cheques de viaje?** |
| Can I pay with this credit card? | **¿Puedo pagar con esta tarjeta de crédito?** |

**M** **MOSQUITOES.** With the occasional exception there are rarely more than a few mosquitoes at a given time, but they survive the year round, and just one can ruin a night's sleep. Few hotels, flats or villas—anywhere on the Mediterranean—have mosquito-proofed windows. Bring your own anti-mosquito devices, whether nets, buzzers, lotions, sprays or incense-type coils that burn all night.

**N** **NEWSPAPERS and MAGAZINES** *(periódico; revista)*. In major tourist areas, most European and British newspapers are sold on the day of publication. Both the Paris-based *International Herald Tribune* and *The New York Times* are on sale. Principal European and American magazines are also available.

Some English-language publications printed in Spain and distributed in Majorca are: *Majorca Daily Bulletin*, a daily newspaper covering national and international news with the accent on Britain and the Balearics; *Guidepost*, a weekly magazine, mostly dealing with the Madrid scene; and *Lookout*, a monthly magazine covering personalities, travel, properties, law and other subjects of interest to foreigners living in or visiting Spain.

On Minorca you'll find a monthly, English-language tourist newspaper, *Roqueta*.

Have you any English-language newspapers? | **¿Tienen periódicos en inglés?**

**P** **PETS.** If you want to take your pet dog or cat along on holiday, you'll need a health and rabies inoculation certificate for the animal, stamped by the Spanish consulate in your own country.

In case of need, a vet may be hard to find. He may also be more accustomed to farm animals than domestic pets. Many hotels don't allow pets, so enquire in advance.

Returning to Great Britain or Eire, your pet will have to go through six months of quarantine for having spent time in a country that is not rabies-free. Both the U.S. and Canada reserve the right to impose quarantine.

**PHOTOGRAPHY.** For the knowledgeable amateur or professional photographer, Spain is a bonanza of picture situations. It is no less so for the once-a-year holiday shutter-bug. But the islands can present a

photographic problem. All those white-walled villages and sparkling **P**
seas, potentially marvellous holiday snaps, fool the electronic eyes on
automatic cameras. Read your camera instruction book in advance,
or have a chat with a camera dealer and show him your equipment.

For beaches, whitewashed houses and other strongly lit scenes, use
incidental readings stopped down, i.e. reduced by one-third or one-
half stop; or follow the instructions with the film. If in doubt, bracket
your exposures—expose above and below the selected exposure—
especially with transparency film. For good results don't shoot between 11 a.m. and 3 p.m. unless there's light cloud to soften the sun.

All popular film makes and sizes are available in Spain. Prices are
generally higher than in the rest of Europe or North America, so it is
advisable to bring a good stock. Polaroid film is particularly expensive.
To get the best results from the black-and-white *Negra* and *Valca,*
you'll need to experiment, especially with processing. The colour
negative film *Negracolor* is fine for family shots. All transparency
film is imported.

If possible always keep film—exposed and unexposed—in a refrig-
erator.

| | |
|---|---|
| I'd like a film for this camera. | **Quisiera un carrete para esta máquina.** |
| a black-and-white film | **un carrete en blanco y negro** |
| a colour-slide film | **un carrete de diapositivas** |
| a film for colour pictures | **un carrete para película en color** |
| 35-mm film | **un carrete treinta y cinco** |
| super-8 | **super ocho** |
| How long will it take to develop (and print) this film? | **¿Cuánto tardará en revelar (y sacar copias de) este carrete?** |
| May I take a picture? | **¿Puedo sacar una fotografía?** |

**POLICE** *(policía).* There are three police forces in Spain: the *Policía
Municipal,* who are attached to the local town hall and usually wear a
blue uniform; the *Cuerpo Nacional de Policía,* a national anti-crime
unit recognized by their brown uniforms; and the *Guardia Civil,* the
national police force wearing patent-leather hats, patrol town and
country.

If you need police assistance, you can call on any one of the three.
Spanish police are efficient, strict and particularly courteous to foreign
visitors.

| | |
|---|---|
| Where's the nearest police station? | **¿Dónde está la comisaría más cercana?** |

119

**PUBLIC HOLIDAYS** (*fiesta*)

| | | |
|---|---|---|
| January 1 | *Año Nuevo* | New Year's Day |
| January 6 | *Epifanía* | Epiphany |
| March 19 | *San José* | St. Joseph's Day |
| May 1 | *Día del Trabajo* | Labour Day |
| July 25 | *Santiago Apóstol* | St. James' Day |
| August 15 | *Asunción* | Assumption |
| October 12 | *Día de la Hispanidad* | Discovery of America Day (Columbus Day) |
| November 1 | *Todos los Santos* | All Saints' Day |
| December 6 | *Día de la Constitución Española* | Constitution Day |
| December 8 | *Inmaculada Concepción* | Immaculate Conception |
| December 25 | *Navidad* | Christmas Day |
| Movable dates: | *Jueves Santo* | Maundy Thursday |
| | *Viernes Santo* | Good Friday |
| | *Lunes de Pascua* | Easter Monday (Catalonia) |
| | *Corpus Christi* | Corpus Christi |

These are only the national holidays of Spain. There are many special holidays for different branches of the economy or different regions. Consult the tourist office in the area where you are staying.

Are you open tomorrow?  **¿Está abierto mañana?**

**R**   **RADIO and TV** (*radio; televisión*). A short-wave set of reasonable quality will pick up all European capitals. Reception of Britain's BBC World Service usually rates from good to excellent, either direct or through their eastern Mediterranean relay station. In the winter, especially mornings and evenings, a good set will pull in the BBC medium and long-wave "Home" programmes.

The Voice of America usually comes through loud and clear, though in Spain the programme is not received 24 hours a day. The Spanish music programme, *segundo programa,* some jazz but mostly classical, is excellent. Majorcan radio stations schedule programmes in English, French, German, Danish and Swedish.

Most hotels and bars have television, usually tuned in to sports—including international soccer and rugby—bull fighting, variety or nature programmes. Broadcasting is in Castilian and Majorcan.

**RELIGIOUS SERVICES** *(servicio religioso)*. The national religion is Roman Catholicism, but other denominations and faiths are represented. On Majorca numerous faiths hold services in English:

Anglican: Núñez de Balboa, 6, Son Armadams, Palma; Sunday.
Baha'i Centre: Avenida Sindical, 50-b, Palma.
Catholic: Church of San Fernando, Carretera Arenal, 303, Las Maravillas; Sunday.
Church of Santa Brígida de Suecia, Apartamentos Impala IV, Palma; Saturday, Sunday and holy days.
Chapel of Inmaculada, Teniente Mulet, 38, El Terreno; Sunday.
Franciscan Seminary, Playa de Palma; Sunday.
Parish Church, El Arenal.
Parish Church, Paguera; Sunday.
Parish Church, Plaza Santa Mónica, San Agustín; Sunday.
Christian Community Church: Calle Murillo, 8, Palma; Sunday.
Christian Science: Calle Monseñor Palmer, 23, Palma; Sunday.
Evangelical Church: Calle Murillo, 16, Palma; Sunday.
Evangelical Pentecostal: Calle Arquitecto Forteza, 18, Palma; Sunday.
Jewish services: Hotel Santa Ana, Cala Mayor; Friday evening.

On Minorca, Anglican services are conducted monthly at Mation and Villa Carlos alternately.

What time is mass/the service?     **¿A qué hora es la misa/el culto?**

**TIME DIFFERENCES.** The Balearics keep the same time as Madrid and the rest of mainland Spain. This chart shows the difference between Spain and some selected cities.

| Los Angeles | Chicago | New York | London | **Majorca** |
|---|---|---|---|---|
| 3 a.m. | 5 a.m. | 6 a.m. | 11 a.m. | **noon** |

As in Great Britain, the United States and Canada, clocks in Spain are turned ahead one hour in spring.

What time is it, please?     **¿Qué hora es, por favor?**     121

**T** **TIPPING.** Since a service charge is normally included in hotel and restaurant bills, tipping is not obligatory. However, it's appropriate to tip porters, bellboys, etc. Follow the chart below for rough guidelines.

| Hotel porter, per bag | minimum 50 ptas. |
|---|---|
| Maid, for extra services | 100–200 ptas. |
| Lavatory attendant | 25–50 ptas. |
| Waiter | 10% (optional) |
| Taxi driver | 10% (optional) |
| Hairdresser/Barber | 10% |
| Tour guide | 10% |

**TOILETS.** There are many expressions for "toilets" in Spanish: *aseos, servicios, W.C., water* and *retretes.* The first two terms are the most common.

Where are the toilets?              **¿Dónde están los servicios?**

**TOURIST INFORMATION OFFICES** *(oficina de turismo).* Spanish National Tourist Offices are maintained in many countries throughout the world:

**British Isles:** 57, St. James's St., London SW1 A1LD; tel. (01) 499-0901

**Canada:** 60 Bloor St. West, Suite 201, Toronto, Ont. M4W 3B8; tel. (416) 961-3131

**U.S.A.:** 845 N. Michigan Ave., Water Tower Place, Chicago, IL 60611; tel. (312) 944-0215
4800 The Galleria, 5085 Westheimer Rd., Houston, TX 77056; tel. (713) 840-7411
8383 Wilshire Boulevard, Suite 960, Beverly Hills, Los Angeles, CA 90211; tel. (213) 658-7188/93
665 5th Ave., New York, NY 10022; tel. (212) 759-8822
Casa del Hidalgo, Hypolita & St. George streets, St. Augustine, FL 32084; tel. (904) 829-6460

The following local tourist offices (normally open from 10 a.m. to 1 p.m. and 4 to 7.30 p.m.) are maintained in Palma de Mallorca:

Oficina de Turismo, Avinguda Rei Jaume III, 10; tel. 71 22 16/
72 40 90

Fomento de Turismo, Carrer de Constitucio, 1; tel. 72 45 37
airport, tel. 26 08 03

On Minorca, there's one at Arco de San Roque, Mahón; tel. 36 37 90

## TRANSPORT

**Buses:** Majorca is well served by bus lines. Destinations are usually clearly marked on the front of the bus. Additional buses operate between Palma and the principal beaches during the summer season.

A return (round-trip) bus ticket is always cheaper than an advertised travel-agency tour.

For information on timetables and fares, ask at a central bus station *(estación central de autobuses)* or at any tourist information office in a coastal resort town.

**Taxis.** Spanish taxis compare very favourably to those in the rest of Europe. It's a good idea to check the fare before you get in. If you take a long trip—for example between two villages—you will be charged a two-way fare whether you make the return journey or not.

All taxis carry price lists in several languages. These lists have been approved by the authorities. If you feel you've been overcharged, you can always ask the driver to show you the list.

**Trains** *(tren)*. Majorca's railway network, Ferrocarriles de Mallorca, will appeal to tourists more for the fun of it than as "efficient" transport. One route crosses the island from Palma to Inca, another narrow-gauge line goes up through magnificent mountain scenery to Sóller (see p. 51).

| | |
|---|---|
| When's the next bus to …? | **¿Cuándo sale el próximo autobús para …?** |
| single (one-way) | **ida** |
| return (round-trip) | **ida y vuelta** |
| What's the fare to …? | **¿Cuánto es la tarifa a …?** |

**WATER.** When Spaniards drink water, it is almost invariably bottled, rather than from the tap. It is quite common to order water brought to one's room. If you're sensitive to a change in water, watch out, too, for the ice cubes in drinks. Water varies enormously in taste and quality, and the bottled variety is good, clean and cheap.

## DAYS OF THE WEEK

| Sunday | **domingo** | Wednesday | **miércoles** |
|--------|-------------|-----------|---------------|
| Monday | **lunes** | Thursday | **jueves** |
| Tuesday | **martes** | Friday | **viernes** |
| | | Saturday | **sábado** |

## MONTHS

| January | **enero** | July | **julio** |
|---------|-----------|------|-----------|
| February | **febrero** | August | **agosto** |
| March | **marzo** | September | **septiembre** |
| April | **abril** | October | **octubre** |
| May | **mayo** | November | **noviembre** |
| June | **junio** | December | **diciembre** |

## NUMBERS

| 0 | **cero** | 18 | **dieciocho** |
|---|----------|----|---------------|
| 1 | **uno** | 19 | **diecinueve** |
| 2 | **dos** | 20 | **veinte** |
| 3 | **tres** | 21 | **veintiuno** |
| 4 | **cuatro** | 22 | **veintidós** |
| 5 | **cinco** | 30 | **treinta** |
| 6 | **seis** | 31 | **treinta y uno** |
| 7 | **siete** | 32 | **treinta y dos** |
| 8 | **ocho** | 40 | **cuarenta** |
| 9 | **nueve** | 50 | **cincuenta** |
| 10 | **diez** | 60 | **sesenta** |
| 11 | **once** | 70 | **setenta** |
| 12 | **doce** | 80 | **ochenta** |
| 13 | **trece** | 90 | **noventa** |
| 14 | **catorce** | 100 | **cien** |
| 15 | **quince** | 101 | **ciento uno** |
| 16 | **dieciséis** | 500 | **quinientos** |
| 17 | **diecisiete** | 1,000 | **mil** |

# SOME USEFUL EXPRESSIONS

| | |
|---|---|
| yes/no | **sí/no** |
| please/thank you | **por favor/gracias** |
| excuse me/you're welcome | **perdone/de nada** |
| where/when/how | **dónde/cuándo/cómo** |
| how long/how far | **cuánto tiempo/ a qué distancia** |
| yesterday/today/tomorrow | **ayer/hoy/mañana** |
| day/week/month/year | **día/semana/mes/año** |
| left/right | **izquierda/derecha** |
| up/down | **arriba/abajo** |
| good/bad | **bueno/malo** |
| big/small | **grande/pequeño** |
| cheap/expensive | **barato/caro** |
| hot/cold | **caliente/frío** |
| old/new | **viejo/nuevo** |
| open/closed | **abierto/cerrado** |
| here/there | **aquí/allí** |
| free (vacant)/occupied | **libre/ocupado** |
| early/late | **temprano/tarde** |
| easy/difficult | **fácil/difícil** |
| Does anyone here speak English? | **¿Hay alguien aquí que hable inglés?** |
| What does this mean? | **¿Qué quiere decir esto?** |
| I don't understand. | **No comprendo.** |
| Please write it down. | **Escríbamelo, por favor.** |
| Is there an admission charge? | **¿Se debe pagar la entrada?** |
| Waiter!/Waitress! | **¡Camarero!/¡Camarera!** |
| I'd like ... | **Quisiera ...** |
| How much is that? | **¿Cuánto es?** |
| Have you something less expensive? | **¿Tiene algo más barato?** |
| Just a minute. | **Un momento.** |
| Help me, please. | **Ayúdeme, por favor.** |
| Get a doctor, quickly. | **¡Llamen a un médico, rápidamente!** |

# Index

An Asterisk (*) next to a page number indicates a map reference. For index to Practical Information, see page 100.

INDEX

178/802 SUD 23